STUDENT UNIT GUIDE

AS Sociology
UNIT 1

AQA

Module 1: Mass Media

Marsh 047424 ones

For Lola

Philip Allan Updates
Market Place
Deddington
Oxfordshire
OX15 0SE

Tel: 01869 338652
Fax: 01869 337590
e-mail: sales@philipallan.co.uk
www.philipallan.co.uk

ISBN 0 86003 878 5

This Guide has been written specifically to support students preparing for the AQA AS Sociology Unit 1 examination. The content has been neither approved nor endorsed by AQA and remains the sole responsibility of the authors.

Printed by Information Press, Eynsham, Oxford

AS Sociology

Contents

Introduction

■ ■ ■

Content Guidance

■ ■ ■

Questions and Answers

Introduction

About this guide

This unit guide is for students following the AQA AS Sociology course. It deals with the Module 1 topic **Mass Media**, which is examined within Unit 1. Although it provides an overview of the main issues within the topic, you will need to be familiar with the detailed aspects of the topic from your lessons and textbooks. There are three sections to this guide:

- **Introduction** — this provides advice on how to make the best use of the guide, guidance on revision and an outline of the assessment aims of AS Sociology. It also helps with advice on how to be successful in the unit test.

- **Content Guidance** — this provides details of what is included in the specification for Mass Media. (The unit test can be about any aspect of mass media, so do not leave any areas out of your revision.) Each topic area examines the core ideas, stating the main points of evaluation and listing the key concepts and thinkers.

- **Questions and Answers** — this shows you the kind of questions you can expect in the unit test. The first five questions are followed by two sample answers (an A-grade and a C-grade response). These are interspersed with examiner comments so that you can see how the marks are allocated. The sixth question is for you to attempt yourself.

How to use the guide

To use this guide to your best advantage, you should refer to the Introduction and Content Guidance sections from the beginning of your study of Mass Media. However, it would not be advisable to attempt the questions until you feel confident with the general area. When you feel ready to address the questions, take each in turn, study it carefully and then answer the different sections. Try to avoid reading the students' responses until you have completed your own. In this way you will get a better idea of where your answer lies in relation to the given responses. You could look at the grade-C answers and, using the examiner's comments as a guide, try to rewrite them to gain higher marks. Use the grade-A answers to compare with your own. Simply reading through them is useful as a revision guide too.

These tasks can be quite intensive and time-consuming, so try to avoid tackling the questions in a short period of time. It is better to focus on one at a time, and spread the workload over several weeks. Answering the questions is a useful way of developing your exam skills, especially by checking that you have addressed the necessary Assessment Objectives (your teacher will help you with these). The whole process should help you with revision for the particular topic area.

The AS specification

The aims of the AS Sociology course are to enable you to:
- acquire knowledge and a critical understanding of contemporary social processes and structures
- appreciate the significance of theoretical and conceptual issues in sociological debate
- understand sociological methodology and a range of research methods
- reflect on your own experience of the social world in which you live
- develop skills that enhance your ability to participate more effectively in adult life

The AQA AS topic of **Mass Media** is designed to give you a sound understanding of the theories of the role of the media and its importance in contemporary society. You will be expected to be familiar with the theories of the role of the mass media and the debate about ownership and control of the media. This will include perspectives on the media, e.g. Marxist (instrumentalist and hegemonic), pluralist/interactionist and feminist theories. You will be expected to discuss issues of representation and stereotyping of different groups based on their social characteristics such as gender, ethnicity, age, sexuality, social class and disability. Another important area is the selection and presentation of news — this will involve you discussing the different perspectives on the media and the process by which news events are socially constructed. It will also involve a discussion of representation and ideology. One of the most controversial issues in any understanding of the mass media is their effect on their audiences. This has been an ongoing debate since the introduction of the first type of mass medium.

Examinable skills

AS Sociology papers are designed to test certain skills. You will find that the Assessment Objectives are common to both AS and A2, although their weighting differs. There are two main examinable skills in the specification and each counts for half of the marks available.

Assessment Objective 1 (AO1) is 'knowledge and understanding'. Knowledge and understanding are linked together, indicating that you must not only demonstrate sociological knowledge but also be able to use it in a meaningful way. Understanding implies that you can select appropriate knowledge and use it in answer to a specific question. The skill of knowledge and understanding covers the following aspects of sociological thought:
- social order
- social control
- social change

- conflict and consensus
- social structure and social action
- macro- and micro-perspectives
- the nature of social facts
- the role of values
- the relationship between sociology and social policy

AS candidates are also required to study two core themes:
- socialisation, culture and identity
- social differentiation, power and stratification

These themes are to be applied to the topic areas in the specification and not tested as separate topics. You will be able to see how these two core themes can be applied to the topic of Mass Media as you read this book.

Assessment Objective 2 (AO2) covers 'identification, analysis, interpretation and evaluation'. You will be expected to show that you can:
- **select and apply** a range of relevant concepts and theories
- **interpret** qualitative and quantitative data
- **identify** significant social trends
- and finally, **evaluate** different theories, arguments and evidence

Although these skills may sound daunting at first, you will soon get used to them and be able to apply them as you begin to think sociologically. For instance, identification means being able to pick out appropriate information, which might simply be describing a trend in a statistical table. You will learn how to distinguish between facts and opinions, to weigh up the strengths and limitations of different theories and research methods, and to analyse the evidence that you have in front of you. The fourth skill in AO2, evaluation, is a very important one — probably the most sophisticated of the sociological skills. It forces you to ask questions such as, 'How reliable are these data?', 'How adequate is this theory today?' and 'From what perspective is this argued?' Clearly, you need to have a grasp of all the other skills to evaluate properly.

In addition to demonstrating the skills in your written work, whether in the examination room or for a homework assignment, you must:
- be well organised so that your arguments are coherent
- show an awareness of the theoretical debates in sociology
- use evidence to support and sustain your arguments and conclusions

Study skills and revision strategies

- Good revision equals good results — you need to spend time revising.
- As well as reading and making notes, read a quality newspaper such as the *Guardian*, the *Independent* or the *Observer* at least once a week. The *Guardian*

has sections dedicated to media, education and society that are of particular sociological interest. They will provide you with contemporary examples that you can refer to in your essays.

- Use the internet. There are now some excellent websites dedicated to AS and A-level Sociology.
- If you do not already subscribe to *Sociology Review*, your school or college library probably does. Read back copies. This magazine is invaluable for keeping you up to date with sociological research and for giving good advice on exams.
- For each of your AS and A2 units, make sure that you know what the examination board specifies as necessary knowledge. Make notes on each of these areas and keep them in a revision folder separate from your class notes.
- Be organised! Make yourself an examination timetable, divided into topics, at least 2 months before the exams start.
- When you finally reach the week(s) of the exams themselves, get a good night's sleep each night. Do *not* stay up until the early hours trying to get in some last-minute revision.
- In the exam, allocate your time carefully. Make sure that you have enough time to write the *two* essays as well as to answer the shorter parts of the question.

The unit test

Mass Media is a Module 1 topic. This module also contains the topics of Families and Households, and Health. The unit test will contain three questions, one on each of the three topics, and you will have to answer one question in the examination time of $1\frac{1}{4}$ hours. The unit as a whole is worth 35% of the AS qualification and $17\frac{1}{2}$% of the total A-level qualification. Each question is marked out of 60, and of the 60 marks, 30 are given to AO1 (knowledge and understanding) and 30 to AO2 (identification, interpretation, analysis and evaluation).

Each question in the examination will feature source material, or 'items' — usually two of them. These are designed to help you by providing information on which you may draw in your answer. It is therefore essential that before attempting to answer any part of the question, you read the items carefully, and continue to refer to them throughout the examination. Sometimes a question will make a specific reference to an item, such as 'With reference to Item A', or 'Using evidence from Item B and elsewhere'. In these cases make sure that you follow the instruction. An easy way of doing this is to say, for example, 'The view referred to in Item A is that ...', 'Item A shows evidence of...' or 'Item A clearly offers a Marxist viewpoint'.

Each question is broken down into a number of parts, usually (a) to (f), each with its own mark allocation. The first series of questions, typically (a) to (d), will together add up to 20 marks, and require short answers. As is usual in such cases, the higher the mark allocation, the more time you would normally need to spend on your answer to gain full marks. Questions (e) and (f) will each be marked out of 20 and will require you to write essay-type answers. The weighting of the skills for these two questions will be different.

Part (e) is weighted towards knowledge and understanding, which carries 14 of the 20 available marks, leaving 6 marks for AO2 skills. This means that in answering this question, you should ensure that you demonstrate appropriate knowledge of socio-logical theories, evidence and concepts. The wording of the question here is likely to be 'Examine the evidence for...' or 'Examine the view that...', so you must not neglect the other skills, especially evaluation. Make sure that you include some critical or evaluative comments at suitable points in your answer.

In part (f) the skills balance is reversed, that is, 14 of the 20 marks are awarded for the skills of identification, interpretation, analysis and evaluation, with 6 marks avail-able for knowledge and understanding. The question should alert you to what you have to do, by asking you to 'evaluate' or 'assess' something.

Content
Guidance

This section outlines the major issues and themes covered in **Mass Media** and provides references to some key studies. Remember, though, that these are offered as guidance only — the lists are neither exhaustive nor exclusive; there are other concepts that are useful and many other studies that are relevant to this topic. With regard to studies, whatever textbook you use will contain sufficient examples for your needs, and your teacher will undoubtedly refer you to others. If you have back copies of *Sociology Review* in your library, you will find a number of useful articles on this area of the course. In addition to sociological research, there are many books and articles in which sociologists discuss their ideas on the mass media. These will be referenced in your textbooks. We would recommend the following websites:

www.theory.org.uk
www.ie.ac.uk/education/centres/ATSS/atss.html
www.sociology.org.uk
www.aber.ac.uk/media

The content of Mass Media falls into the following main sections:
- **Theories of the role of the media in society**
- **The ownership and control debate**
- **Making the news: selection and presentation**
- **Representations of age, social class, ethnicity, gender, sexuality and disability**
- **Audiences and the effects of the media**
- **Media and ideology**

When you have covered all these areas you will have completed the topic. The core themes are integrated within the topic and not dealt with separately.

Theories of the role of the media in society

Instrumentalist or classical Marxist approach

- Instrumentalist Marxists argue that there is a strong relationship between owner-ship and control of the media. Owners of media companies or corporations use their powerful positions to control media content and output. As we will see, instrumentalists argue that the content of the media is biased in favour of dominant groups and the media are used to maintain the status quo.
- The economic base, or infrastructure, is seen as responsible for shaping all the other social institutions. It determines the nature of the institutions in the super-structure such as the law, religion, family, education and the media. These act to legitimate or maintain the position of the powerful.
- The dominant or ruling ideas of any historical period are those of the ruling class, and the promotion of these ideas is heavily dependent on media institutions. In this way the media operate as part of the ideological state apparatus (ISA) to produce messages reinforcing the ideology of the bourgeoisie.
- The media concentrate on conservative ideas and ridicule radical or revolutionary ones. Groups which threaten dominant ideas — such as the anti-capitalist movement — are often portrayed in a negative light, and by providing a steady diet of trivia to audiences, media owners divert attention away from the real issues of importance in society.
- The media are engaged in encouraging consumption through commercial adver-tising. The media relay messages that help to keep capitalism going.
- This perspective stresses the strength of the media as an influence on a passive and impressionable audience.

Evaluation

- + This approach acknowledges the importance of theory to the understanding of the media.
- + It draws our attention to political and economic interests.
- + The media are placed firmly within the power structure of society.
- + The importance of social class in relation to media ownership is emphasised.
- − The approach is overly deterministic and takes little or no account of the power of audiences to make choices concerning their media consumption.
- − In assuming that proprietors have direct control over the media content, it fails to show how this is manageable given the size and extent of media conglomerations.

- Pluralists would argue that there is no conspiracy among owners to control audiences and stress the power of consumers to make choices about what they read, watch and listen to.

Key concepts

infrastructure; superstructure; dominant ideas; legitimation; ideological state apparatus; ownership and control

Key thinkers

Althusser, Miliband, Marcuse

Hegemonic (structuralist Marxist) theory

- Developed by Antonio Gramsci (1891–1937) as a challenge to the economic determinism of instrumentalist Marxism.
- According to Gramsci, hegemony meant 'moral and philosophical leadership' whereby the subject classes would not simply accept the rule of the dominant class by force or coercion, but had to be won over by ideological leadership. The working class comes to believe these powerful ideas to be right.
- The media portray a rather limited image of the world. This is known as the *Weltanschauung* — the worldview of white male middle-class media professionals, which reflects to audiences the world that they know. Other groups such as black youth, single mothers, trade unionists, feminists and welfare claimants are marginalised and seen as a threat to the social consensus. Audiences come to accept the dichotomy of 'us' as respectable and 'them' as problematic and so are more easily won over.
- These dominant ideas make sense of the social world but are neither static nor fixed. Ideas are always contested and struggled over. The ruling class has to take into account new situations and offer new concessions. Once ideas become fixed, they are in danger of becoming old-fashioned and will lose their power.

Evaluation

+ Hegemonic theory challenges the idea that the audience is passive and manipulated by the dominant group.
+ Two British academic centres in particular have produced a wealth of evidence on the ideological role of the media. These are the Glasgow University Media Group (GMG) and the Centre for Contemporary Cultural Studies (CCCS). They have been especially interested in the processes of news production and the relationship between ideology and representation.
+ The research conducted by the GMG since *Bad News* in 1976 has been highly controversial and has been the subject of a great deal of criticism, not least from journalists and broadcasters themselves. However, the research has shown the ways in which news presentation is socially constructed in favour of dominant groups.

- If culture is always tied to dominant ideas, then it would be difficult to explain alternative and independent media.
- Hegemony may be seen as a variation of Althusser's analysis of ideological state apparatuses.

Key concepts

winning consent; ideology; marginalisation, struggle, primary definers

Key thinkers

Gramsci, Hall, GMG, CCCS

Pluralism

- Pluralists reject the Marxist analysis of the nature of power and control in society.
- They argue that power is not concentrated among the bourgeoisie who manipulate the media to exert ideological control but among a wider range of interest groups. As a result, the media reflect diverse views and opinions of these competing groups.
- In contrast to the instrumentalist view, which sees the viewer/reader/listener as essentially passive in relation to media output, pluralists stress the ability of members of the public to choose the media product they want.
- The media have to respond to public demand. Changes in the media are brought about because the public is no longer satisfied with existing media products, i.e. viewing/readership figures decline, so programmes are dropped from schedules and newspapers cease publication.
- Pluralists argue that the wide range of newspapers and magazines available, the differences between the five terrestrial television channels and the wide range of radio broadcasting all go to show that choice is considerable for the consumer of the media. Left-wing journals are available on the newsstands even though people might choose not to buy them.
- Satellite and digital television offer many channels, giving viewers immense choice.

Evaluation

- + Audiences are not passive recipients of media messages, but are able to make choices about what they watch, read and listen to.
- + This approach allows us to see that the media do not speak with a single voice. Even taking one medium such as newspapers, we can see that events are given very different treatment by tabloids and broadsheet press.
- + There is bias in the media, but audiences are able to recognise it so the media lose the power of manipulation.
- − Media diversity does not in reality offer wide-ranging choices. There will be increasing concentration of ownership, especially with Rupert Murdoch taking control of digital television broadcasting.

- Journalists are closely vetted before recruitment so that very few dissident voices are heard.
- Newspapers which support more extreme, left-of-centre viewpoints are as dependent on advertising revenue as those which support more conservative positions, but as their circulations are smaller than the rest of newspapers, they are less secure.
- Pluralists ignore the possibility that we may not get what media we want but may learn to want what we are given.

Key concepts

choice; autonomy; plurality; diversity; selection

Key thinkers

Whale

Feminist perspectives

We can broadly identify three feminist approaches, all of which share a focus on gender as the way in which social reality and mediated reality are structured for us and experienced by us.

Liberal feminism

- Liberal feminists adopt a reformist approach which sees more equal gender relations being brought about by equal opportunities policies and affirmative action programmes.
- Much of their work has been through quantitative content analysis, largely focused on advertisements, soap operas and dramas, which shows that women appear less frequently than men, less often in main dramatic roles (although there are variations across genres, with soaps being an important arena for women's characterisations), and in limited roles.
- The general finding is that sex-role stereotyping remains a major feature of television programming, both here and in the USA, and that in these programmes women are confined to lives that are centred on domesticity and personal, familial relationships. 'Symbolic annihilation' of women was the common finding from content analyses. Significant social changes in women's lives have been only partially reflected by the media.
- The liberal feminist position maintains that over time media representation of women will catch up with their actual social position and the media will present a more realistic view.

Evaluation

+ This is the first approach to research the 'hard data' on gender representations.
- It does not investigate the power relations between men and women.

Radical feminism

- This approach looks at the effect of patriarchy on women. Patriarchy is a system whereby men either directly or indirectly dominate or oppress women.
- Research done by radical feminists has revealed the darker side of family life such as domestic and sexual violence, exposed the exploitation of women by the pornography industry and, more recently, examined the increasingly popular international 'sex tourism' and sex trafficking.
- At its extreme, radical feminism rejects all-male society and considers the only way for women to be liberated is by segregation, usually in the form of lesbian separatism. There are relatively few studies of the media from this perspective, but there have been some studies into pornography.
- Strategies for media work suggested by this approach include women-only communication productions. Women are encouraged to produce their own media products essentially by setting up collective community organisations.

Evaluation

+ This is the first perspective to examine how pornography exploits women and children.
− Radical feminists are small in number and believe that a women-only media would be possible. This is rather idealistic and largely impracticable.

Socialist (Marxist) feminism

- This approach does not focus exclusively on gender, but incorporates analyses of social class, ethnicity, sexual preference, age and disability into the debate.
- Some analyses also place ideology at the centre of the debate. The theory remains focused on social class as the key factor in gender relations.
- The media are seen as ideological apparatuses that represent the essential rightness of capitalism as a social system; within this framework socialist feminists focus on the ways in which gender is constructed through language and imagery.
- Research in this area has tended to be semiological, that is, looking at the meanings of signs and the underlying messages of the texts.

Evaluation

+ The approach links feminist ideas to Marxist theory and examines the importance of ideology.
− It seems to over-emphasise the importance of class at the expense of other factors such as ethnicity.
− Theorists assume that all will be well after the capitalist revolution occurs.

Key concepts

gender; patriarchy; symbolic annihilation; sex-role stereotyping

Key thinkers

Dworkin, Tuchman, Gill, Brett and Cantor, Meehan, Sancier, Ferguson, McRobbie

Postmodernism

- The earlier theories are seen as metanarratives or 'big stories'.
- In terms of the mass media, postmodernists have challenged notions of the audience as essentially passive and easily manipulated. Instead, they argue that we live in an increasingly media-saturated society in which individuals use media images to construct their identities.
- Mass media are central to the postmodern condition because what we now take as 'real' is to a large extent what the media tell us is real. We are bombarded from all sides by cultural signs and images in all aspects of our media.
- According to Baudrillard (1983), we have entered the world of 'simulacra' — signs that function as copies or models of real objects or events. In the postmodern era, we are engulfed by information so that the distinction between reality and its image creates a condition of hyperreality.
- Strinati (1995) argues that the mass media are highly significant in the development of a postmodern society in the following ways:

(1) Breakdown of the distinction between culture and society

Traditional theories of the media assumed that the role of the media was to act as a mirror to the world, but postmodernists say it is no longer possible to separate media from that reality. Postmodern theory focuses upon consumption patterns as providers of our identities.

(2) Emphasis on style at the expense of substance

'Images dominate reality' (Harvey, 1989). Here the argument is that we increasingly consume images and signs for their own sake rather than for a sense of usefulness. We buy on the basis of labels and packaging more than for the clothes and goods inside.

(3) Breakdown of the distinction between art and popular culture

Postmodern culture emphasises playfulness and irony in art and architecture, and makes it very difficult to separate art from popular culture (e.g. Pop Art of the 1960s). Advertisers have used art and classical music to sell products and opera arias have introduced international sporting events.

(4) Confusion over time and space

Traditional notions of time and space have been undermined by satellite broadcasting which has produced instantaneous images and information. We live in a global village where many share similar consumption patterns irrespective of their own culture. Internet communication has shrunk the world.

(5) Decline of metanarratives

Postmodernism casts doubt on the ability of any sociological theory to explain history or to account for power relations in contemporary society. Postmodernists have been particularly critical of Marxism for its attempt to explain social change by using historical materialism and for its emphasis on inevitable progress. The collapse of the Soviet Union and the subsequent rise of capitalism in Eastern Europe have shaken the foundations of orthodox Marxism.

Evaluation

+ Underlying the postmodernist approach is a reluctance to accept that there is one truth. The 'big stories' of history are delusions. Postmodernism celebrates relativism.

+ Postmodernists reject the idea of guaranteed social progress and view society as fragmented, diverse and without clear structures.

+ Postmodernism points to the central position of the media not only in everyday life, but in the very process of constructing our cultural identities.

+ Postmodern images in art and media are playful, ironic and irreverent.

− Postmodernism ignores current media debates surrounding:
  - ownership and control
  - effects of the media
  - bias in the news
  - differential access to the media

− Postmodernism is itself in danger of becoming a new metanarrative. It is highly critical of grand theories such as Marxism, yet it offers its own theory of society as replacement.

− It ignores the continued importance of different cultural and economic circumstances of individuals in the creation of identities.

− The audience is credited with the ability to recognise cultural references in media texts. However, this may simply be another form of media literacy that could be understood as a form of cultural capital.

Key concepts

metanarratives; globalisation, simulacra, hyperreality; popular culture

Key thinkers

Jameson, Lyotard, Baudrillard, Harvey

The ownership and control debate

The theoretical positions of Marxism and pluralism have relevance for a key debate in the topic of the Mass Media, that of ownership and control. The question raised is whether ownership of the media by the media 'barons' implies that they have control over the output of their industries. The concepts of allocative and operational control help to clarify the relationship between ownership and control.

- **Allocative control** means that an individual or group has power to define the overall goals of the organisation and controls its financial policies. This is the most significant form of control as it allows only a particular group to make the major decisions for the organisation.

- **Operational control** is much more a matter of day-to-day control. Once funds have been allocated, media professionals such as editors and producers make decisions about their effective use. Their decisions about output are likely to be influenced by agenda-setting and market appeal (i.e. audience ratings).

Marxist-instrumentalists

- Ownership of the media has become increasingly concentrated and the views expressed are essentially conservative. Key concepts are concentration and conglomeration.
- Media corporations are global, but are still largely owned by individuals such as Murdoch and Berlusconi.
- The media simply serve to legitimate ruling interest groups; they maintain the power of the owners of the means of production.
- Managers only have discretion within the framework set by owners and therefore have limited power.
- Owners share similar social backgrounds and therefore similar interests. They are typically members of a privileged ruling class and run their organisations according to their perceived interests.
- Media ownership can increase political influence too. Berlusconi used his media empire to support his political campaign for premiership of Italy in 1994. He allowed his anchormen to state publicly that they would vote for him in the election, which was illegal.
- Close relationships between political leaders and media barons make media bias very likely. Murdoch was a close political ally of Thatcher, and has become an ally of Blair.

Structuralist/hegemonic Marxists

- Those who adopt this position argue that the sheer size of the media corporations would make it physically impossible for owners to have hands-on control over the day-to-day operations.
- Media professionals control the output of media industries. As they have been socialised into the profession, they understand what makes the news and what makes good television.
- Media professionals are overwhelmingly white, middle-class, middle-aged men with a consensual view of the world. The ideologies that underpin media products are essentially theirs.
- Although their position is Marxist, hegemonic theorists do not see audiences as being easily manipulated; they see them as actively engaged in making sense of media communication.

Pluralists

- Pluralists do not see ownership and control as necessarily or inevitably connected.
- For them, power is not held by a small ruling elite group, but is dispersed among many different groups in society.

- They accept that there is concentration of ownership, but argue that those who are large shareholders simply do not have the time to be involved in the day-to-day operations of the production process.
- Pluralists also see the possibility of any number of people being able to control media enterprises, including the consumer.
- Ultimately, the consumer is in the 'driving seat'. Audiences are active and make decisions over what to watch, read or listen to.
- For pluralists, it makes no difference who owns the media because audiences make the most important decisions.

Making the news: selection and presentation

- Mass media provide us with most of our information about the world. We learn about local, national and international affairs from our newspapers, radios and televisions.
- News production is a complex process of selection, filtering and editing.
- Newspapers get their stories from many sources, not just from the journalists employed by the papers, and it is these sources that help create the type of news that gets produced.
- Because there is more news than any newspaper has room for, all stories have to compete for space and it is the editor's and senior journalists' job to decide which stories to focus on. Editorial meetings are held throughout the day, and some stories are inevitably dropped.
- News comes from various sources: reporters at the scene, foreign correspondents, other media such as television, satellite and video, computer links to other papers, global news agencies and home news agencies. This still does not explain how news items are selected for broadcasting and publication. This is where **news values** come into the process.

News values

- For any item to become 'newsworthy', it has to pass through a selection process — that is, be filtered through a particular set of criteria. Galtung and Ruge (1973) called these criteria 'news values'.
- Both practical and social factors play a part. Practical factors include the timing of an event and the amount of space available in the newspaper or time available in the television news slot.
- Social factors form a framework or pattern within which journalists select items deemed most appropriate.

The following factors form the set of news values:

- **Immediacy or frequency:** this is the time span taken for the event to appear. If the event fits with the timing of the news media, it is more likely to be included.
- **Importance:** normally this means reference to elite nations and/or elite people. National leaders of significant countries will usually make news.
- **Clarity of events:** audiences prefer new items that are easy to understand. If stories are complex they are less likely to be covered.
- **Cultural relevance and proximity:** McLurg's Law shows the way that some foreign news is covered. If a disaster occurs, it will be reported if there is one of our nationals involved or if it is seen as having specific relevance to us. McLurg's ratio of relevance is that one Briton is equal in newsworthiness to 1,000 Africans and 50 French people.
- **Expectedness and unexpectedness:** although these two factors may seem contra-dictory, they are not. An event which is unexpected, such as a disaster of some kind, will be reported, but similarly when an event has gained news value it will continue to be reported because we become familiar with it.
- **Composition:** sometimes an event that seems to have little significance is reported in order to redress an imbalance in the news. If several major international events have been reported, a small national item will be put in to counter-balance them.

Other factors that affect news production:

- **Personalisation:** this usually occurs in relation to politics, when the actions of individual political leaders are taken to stand for political action.
- **Negativity:** bad news usually makes good news. A disaster, war, famine or crash where many people are injured will make the news.

If an event has several of these values, it is highly likely that we will hear about it. In the light of these criteria it is easy to see how the events of 11 September 2001 made global news.

Evaluation

- Boyd-Barrett (1995) argues that the sets of values identified are not explored. For example, the criteria emerge from the worldview of media professionals and need to be examined.

Agenda-setting

- Editors, journalists and producers together decide which items are worthy of making up the television news bulletins or being included in the press. They bring our attention to certain issues, build up public images of political figures and suggest what the viewers, listeners and readers should think about and know about.
- Audiences are presented with a small selection of items as if they are the most significant news of the day, without any suggestion that they are simply constructed by news personnel. We are told not what to think, but what to think *about*.

Gatekeeping

- Gatekeeping is an important process that helps us to understand why some items are allowed as news, whereas others may never get onto the news agenda. This is especially significant in times of social crisis such as war, when 'bad news' is withheld in case it has a negative effect on public morale. (For example, the number of casualties of a war or conflict may be withheld if a general election is approaching.)
- There is no such thing as an impartial news story. Every story tells you something about the values of the news organisation by its length and where it appears in the newspaper (front page or one of the inside pages) or the television news running order.

Evaluation

- News producers are not all powerful. Even though ultimately the news editor or individual journalist does have the 'real' power of editing, prioritising or sensationalising an issue, those who act as sources of information for the media can use PR strategies to get what they want across.
- Pluralists argue that the variety of news outlets guarantees that several different voices are heard.
- Public service broadcasting has a legal responsibility to remain impartial in political debates.
- The public may not necessarily share the same views or values on news events, as those of media professionals.
- The media do not always speak with the same voice.

Key concepts

access; ideology

Key thinkers

White

Inferential structures of news production

Hegemonic Marxists argue that:
- The media routinely operate in relation to news using a set of organisational frameworks and assumptions that structure stories about events within dominant interpretations.
- Journalists make these events accessible to the audiences. Audiences are assumed to share a common stock of knowledge about the world, and so have access to shared meanings about society.
- Routine day-to-day organisation of news production involves several different kinds of news source: the public, official sources, news agencies and other media.

- Journalists usually take their news from reliable, generally official news sources and, owing to increased pressure to meet critical print deadlines, they become increasingly reliant on these sources rather than going out into the field and doing more investigative work.
- News needs to be seen to be impartial, balanced and objective. This is, of course, formally structured in television news production, but with the press, journalists often refer to official sources as if they are factual and objective.
- Official sources become essential in the process of news production. They may be government spokespeople, managers, leaders of industry, police officers etc. — what they have in common is privileged access to the media. They are the **primary definers** of the situation and are therefore very significant in how we, as the audience, come to understand the news events.

Evaluation

- Pluralists would argue that there is no conspiracy at work in news production.
- They would say that there are many sources available to the media professionals and that they are in competition to provide our news.
- They would also argue that the media do not speak with one voice.

Key concepts

worldview; ideology

Key thinkers

Hall, GMG, Schlesinger

Representation

The media communicate with their audiences through the process of representation by using familiar signs and symbols. In this way the media represent events to us as if they are natural.

Representation focuses on some groups more than others and is inevitably ideological. The media give us images of particular groups that can have substantial effects on how those groups experience the world, and how others treat them. It is important to remember that representation is a **process** by which some groups are portrayed as well as the end-product of that process.

Gender

- Traditional feminist critiques of the media have concentrated on the relative absence of women from significant areas of the media, such as news and current affairs, political debates and sports reporting. They have also highlighted the demeaning portrayal of women in the media, particularly in the tabloid press, and the reinforcement of sex-role stereotyping in advertising.

- Gaye Tuchman (1978) argued that the media symbolically annihilate women. Women appear far less often on television compared to men and when they do, the roles they occupy are very limited and/or negative. She claimed that the media frequently condemn or trivialise women's activities and experiences.

- However, liberal feminists would argue that the picture has changed and women are occupying more roles than in the past.

- Television generally over-emphasises certain roles for women — in particular, the sexual and the domestic. This decorative sexual role is a highly passive one in which women are objectified — they are seen as objects of the 'male gaze' (Mulvey, 1975).

- Meehan's analysis of American soap operas (1983) concluded that there were only ten character types for women in these shows. She named them: the Imp, the Goodwife, the Harpy, the Bitch, the Victim, the Decoy, the Siren, the Courtesan, the Witch and the Matriarch.

- Research into the portrayal of women in advertising has found that there is still significant sex-role stereotyping. Most work settings involve men, while domestic settings mainly involve women.

- Cumberbatch's (1990) study showed that no significant changes in the representation of women in advertising had taken place. In general, men still outnumbered women on screen by a ratio of nearly 2:1. With respect to voice-overs, over 89% used a male voice. In terms of occupational roles, men were twice as likely as women to be portrayed in some kind of paid employment (30% of men, 16% of women). Cumberbatch concluded that, 'women exist in what is essentially a man's world'.

- Findings from Sherman and Dominick's work (1986) showed that the roles of women in music videos were severely limited. Typical roles were submissive, physically attractive and sensual.

- Vincent, Davis and Boruszkowski (1987) also conducted research into gender portrayal in music videos on MTV. They concluded that sexism was a very prominent feature of the videos. In general, women were portrayed in a decorative role, and in 10% of the videos analysed, women were shown to be victims of male violence.

- Feminists argue that women's magazines reinforce the idea that being thin is associated with good health and attractiveness. Rosalind Coward (1984) argues that advertising encourages women to adopt a view of their bodies as a 'project' and one, rather like DIY, which can always be improved upon.

- Recent concern has been expressed over a possible relationship between representations of women's bodies and consequent links with both eating disorders and distorted body images of young women.

- Feminists generally have been highly critical of many of the representations of women by the media, but they also acknowledge that the media are not solely responsible for gender-role stereotyping. Other institutions such as the family, education and religion also contribute.

+ Feminist studies using quantitative content analysis were the first to demonstrate that women were symbolically annihilated by the media.
+ They have shown that the representation of women in contemporary media products such as computer games and music videos remains limited to the decorative or sexual.
- The reliance on quantitative content analysis by feminists has been criticised. Many sociologists assert that this technique is highly subjective and unsophisticated.

Key concepts

symbolic annihilation; sexism; decoration; stereotyping; domestic; feminism; content analysis, male gaze

Key thinkers

Tuchman, Cumberbatch, Meehan, Mulvey, Coward

Ethnicity

On television, the representation of ethnic minorities has been stereotypical, limited especially to sport, music and entertainment, and crime.

Their portrayal by the media has been categorised in the following ways (Alvarado et al., 1987):

The exotic

- Hall (1990) referred to the 'white eye', which assumes that the dominant or preferred readings of audiences will be from the point of view of whites.
- The inferential structures of media production (the ways in which media professionals operate) communicate a taken-for-granted or institutional racism.
- In this way, ethnic groups are seen as the 'other', often represented as wondrous and strange. Their rituals, dress, language, artefacts and food are not understood as parts of complex cultural and social formations, but are seen as exotic.

The dangerous

- This is the view that minority groups pose a threat to the rest of society — as immigrants, muggers and, more recently, asylum seekers. The latter are seen as taking advantage of Britain and in some cases belonging to terrorist groups. Van Djik (1991) demonstrated underlying racism in press reporting.

The humorous

- In the early 1970s, race was a major vehicle for comedy. As Stuart Hall (1981) explained, comedy programmes did not simply have black characters in them: they were 'about race'.

- These programmes neutralised black people as threats to the country by making them the butt of racist jokes.
- However, there is evidence of more recent positive change.

The pitied

- Representation of ethnic groups as victims, usually of 'natural' disasters, such as famine, drought or flood, but also of conflicts, has become commonplace.
- Images of children are often used by charities to elicit our sympathy. The early footage of the Ethiopian famine victims, which gave rise to the first Band Aid charity concerts, was focused on the plight of the children.

Evaluation

+ Pluralists would argue that the representation of ethnic minority groups has become more positive. There are many more black presenters on television than in earlier years.
+ Black athletes and musicians are portrayed very positively.
− Since the terrorist attacks on New York and Washington on 11 September 2001 the portrayal of some Muslim groups has been less positive.
− Ethnic minorities are still under-represented as producers, researchers and writers.

Key concepts

racism; stereotyping; 'white eye'; inferential structures of racism; institutional racism

Key thinkers

Hall, Hartmann and Husband, Troyna, Alvarado, van Dijk

Disability

- There has been little research specifically into images of disability, but it is clear that the disabled constitute another marginalised group.
- Research from the Broadcasting Standards Commission (1999) showed that people with disabilities appeared in only 7% of the programmes sampled. In the sample, disabled males outnumbered females 3:1 with 1:10 from an ethnic minority. There were more disabled people in US productions than in British.
- Longmore (1987) identified characteristics of representations of the disabled on television. Disability was associated with evil, a loss of humanity, total dependency and a lack of self-determination, and the disabled were represented as 'monsters' or as maladjusted. Where positive characteristics were shown, the disabled were seen as courageous in overcoming adversity; alternatively, disability was portrayed as a substitute gift. Disability was sometimes linked with a lack of sexual control.
- In another research study, Cumberbatch and Negrine (1992) looked at televised dramatic fiction and characters' attitudes to the disabled. They found that the main attitudes were sympathy, condescension, respect and attraction, but these latter two were expressed more frequently towards the able-bodied.

- Disabled people are rarely, if ever, shown on television as an integral part of everyday life. Where they appear, they are referenced within the framework of their disability, not as individuals who happen to have a disability.

Key concepts

body fascism; stereotyping; social construction

Key thinkers

Longmore, Cumberbatch and Negrine, Shakespeare

Social class

There have been very few studies of the representation of class in the media. We also have to understand that social class is not a straightforward category; different theorists have different views of class. The categories referred to here are upper, middle and working class.

- Social inequality, unless in developing countries, is rarely examined.
- There is an under-representation of working-class people on television in family drama and sitcoms.
- In the USA, the majority of leading characters are middle-class males. Jhally and Lewis found that between 1971 and 1989, 90% of US television characters were middle class.
- Presenters and experts in the UK media tend to be middle-class males.
- On UK television, working-class representation is mainly on soaps, crime and hospital dramas, as offenders and patients, and in programmes like the BBC's *The Royle Family*.
- In non-fictional programmes, working-class people get a poor representation. Studies of coverage of industrial disputes suggest that working-class employees are portrayed as problematic. Working-class youths, especially if they are black, are also seen as troublesome and are often the subject of moral panic. Welfare claimants have been similarly stereotyped as 'scroungers'.

Evaluation

- **Instrumentalist Marxists** might explain this under-representation of the working class as manipulation of media content by the capitalist class or their representatives, the owners. By displaying aspirational (middle-class) lifestyles they can encourage more consumption and thereby reinforce middle-class values in order to maintain the status quo.
- **Hegemonic Marxists** might explain the under-representation as an expression of the consensual view of the world held by the middle-class males who control the media. They see some groups as a threat to the consensus and therefore treat them as marginal. This is another example of the inferential structures of media production.

Key concepts

stereotyping; marginalisation; moral panics; content analysis

Key thinkers

GMG, Golding, Glennon and Butsch, Jhally and Lewis

Sexuality

- Examining the representation of sexuality by the media is complex because we cannot necessarily tell a person's sexuality in the same way that we can identify markers of sex and race.
- Dyer (1993) argued that it was possible to identify four stereotypes of gays represented in films: in-betweenism, macho, the sad young man and lesbian feminism.
- **In-betweenism** is characterised by the gay types of queen and dyke, where the 'queen' is portrayed as effeminate, 'not a real man', while the dyke is very masculine, 'butch' and 'not a real woman'. **Macho** is only applied to gay men, and is an exaggerated form of masculinity such as the body-builder. The **sad young man** emerged in American cinema in the 1960s. He signified a troubled adolescent, unsure of his sexuality. The image of the sad young man has recently been used by advertisers to sell men's fashion and cosmetics. **Lesbian feminism** has been portrayed as a culture that is closer to nature and naturalness.
- Over the past two decades, there has been a significant change in the representation of both gays and lesbians on television and in magazines. *Queer As Folk* (Channel 4) followed the lives of three gay men, and many soap operas have included gay characters and gay relationships. Magazines such as *Attitude* and *Gay Times* target gay audiences, which also make up the readership of many mainstream lifestyle magazines. However, gay and lesbian characters remain marginal.

Key concepts

marginalisation; homophobia

Key thinkers

Dyer, Sanderson

Age

- Representation of age in the media is linked to the ideology of ageism, that is, negative feelings towards, and/or discriminatory behaviour against, a person or group because of their age. Underlying ideological assumptions about age rely on biological characteristics and ignore the social construction of age. Children are presented mainly as innocents, adolescents are presented as rebellious and the elderly are portrayed as sexless and helpless.
- Content analyses of representations of the elderly on American television show that women are under-represented compared with men, and that traditional sex-role stereotyping prevails. Representations of elderly women of all classes tend to be affected by ageist assumptions.

- Adolescents or 'youths' tend to be represented in a negative way. They have been the folk devils of several moral panics, e.g. as drug-takers, hooligans and muggers.
- Children are seen as innocent or mischievous — they are vulnerable when victims of strangers, but are represented as holding considerable 'pester-power' in persuading parents to buy products for them. In extreme cases, where children kill other children, they have been portrayed as 'evil'.

Key concepts

Ageism; youth subcultures; folk devils; stereotyping; social construction

Key thinkers

Alvarado et al., Hall, Pearson, Young, Medved, Cohen

Audiences and the effects of the media

There are many different ways in which researchers have analysed possible effects of media on their audiences. Attention has been paid to the effect of cinema, the press and, especially, television on aggressive behaviour, anti-social behaviour, pro-social behaviour, attitudes, prejudice, sexual habits, morality and so on. The debate is polarised between a media-centric approach which assumes that media are all-powerful and audiences are weak and easily manipulated, and an opposing view which sees audiences as all-powerful and attributes little or no power to the mass media.

Media strong, audience weak: the hypodermic syringe model

The 'hypodermic syringe' model was based upon earlier studies of persuasion and propaganda which took for granted the idea that mass audiences, such as crowds, were easily manipulated. The belief that the new mass media had the potential for enormous influence characterised much of the period up to the 1940s. However, the basic assumption of powerful media is still held, especially as a commonsensical view of the media. For instance, whenever an event takes place which offends the public sense of morality, there are people looking to scapegoat the media for encouraging the underlying behaviour.

A classic example of the powerful influence of the media was Orson Welles's radio broadcast in the USA in 1938 dramatising H. G. Wells's novel *The War of the Worlds*. The adaptation was so convincing in its apparently factual reporting of an invasion of New Jersey by Martians that it generated mass hysteria in many American states.

Direct effects: Bandura and Walters

Behaviourist psychologists working under laboratory conditions conducted much of the direct effects research in the 1960s. Bandura and his associates examined the relationship between imitation and aggression. In a series of experiments using a mallet and a 'Bobo' doll (a large inflatable doll with a rounded base, which rolls back when hit), they tested the reactions of groups of children as they were watching films of an adult hitting the Bobo doll. The children were then left alone with an identical doll and a mallet and their behaviour was observed.

The two-step flow hypothesis

With their book, *Personal Influence* (1955), Elihu Katz and Paul Lazarsfeld changed the perspective of media research for a decade. They were able to show that rather than being made up of isolated individuals with no power to defend themselves against the media, the audience contained active individuals who influenced others. These were 'opinion leaders' whose personal characteristics enabled them to persuade other people to their viewpoint. Katz and Lazarsfeld maintained that although the link between exposure and decision-making was a complex one, the opinion leaders' greater exposure to the media informed their decision-making. The research focused on specific areas where opinion leaders were influential on other people; these were shopping, fashion, going to the cinema and ideas about current affairs and politics.

Audience needs and satisfactions: the uses and gratifications approach

The uses and gratifications approach was mainly concerned with choice, reception and response within the audience. Audience members were perceived as being more active, motivated in their media use and aware of their own social and psychological needs. These 'needs' can be grouped under the following headings:

- diversion and escape (from the routine of domesticity)
- personal relationships (as topics of conversation and 'company' for the isolated person)
- personal identity (as a means of comparison with oneself)
- surveillance (gaining information about the world)

Herzog's research on women listeners to radio serials (1944) showed that women gained satisfactions such as emotional release, vicarious pleasures and identification with characters from their regular listening.

Evaluation
+ The audience is seen as more actively involved with the media.
+ The audience is seen as differentiated (for example, by gender) rather than assumed to be homogeneous.
+ It allows us to see that some media are used differently by different audience groups.
− The model fails to examine why people have particular needs.
− It fails to see that the needs may be created by the media.
− It ignores the sociocultural background of audiences.

Reinforcement theory

Rather than researchers asking what the media do to their audiences, this approach asks what we do with the media. The focus ceases to be on the media, shifting to the social factors that operate to influence the individual. Halloran (1970) directed attention away from a media-centric approach to one where the media were seen in a social context.

Evaluation
+ This approach sees that television has an important reinforcing influence, but one which affects individuals in different ways depending upon the social circumstances in which individuals are placed.
+ The role of television as an agent of socialisation is emphasised, but within the context of other important agencies, like the family and peer groups.
− The approach does not allow us to make predictions as to which media texts will be used as reinforcers by specific individuals. We can therefore only analyse the reinforcement effect after it has taken place.

Structuring reality: towards the active audience

Cultivation analysis

Cultivation analysis, as put forward by Gerbner and others, sees the crucial importance of television in daily life — so much so that it dominates our 'symbolic environment'. What Gerbner means by this is that some people in the audience come to believe in the reality or 'mediated reality' presented by television rather than their own personal experiences of reality.

The central assumptions of this theory are that the media represent the world in highly selective, stereotyped and distorted ways. These images are cumulative, so that heavy viewers are subjected to this mediated view of the world and assume it is a reflection of the world outside their windows.

Evaluation

+ This approach attempts to differentiate audience responses and emphasises an active audience.
+ It considers the differences in media influence between light and heavy viewers.
− Reinterpretation of Gerbner et al.'s work demonstrates other methodological problems. Measuring long-term attitudinal effects of the media on individuals is very difficult because so many of our attitudes result from early socialisation.
− It would be impossible for researchers to quantify the possible effects of the media in isolation from other social influences.

Reception analysis: media weak, audience active

This approach does not look for an effects relationship as such. It is more concerned with the way audiences read media texts and is popular among cultural studies theorists and researchers. It attempts to demonstrate how we make sense of the messages and images of popular culture through a process of interpretation. Most reception studies use an **ethnographic** approach, using qualitative methods such as in-depth interviewing, participant observation and group discussions, e.g. Hobson (1982); Morley (1980, 1988); Buckingham (1993). Some, like Ang (1985), have used viewers' letters. These researchers have all attempted to explore the interpretations of the texts as understood by their audiences.

Evaluation

+ The approach sees the audience as active and media-literate.
+ Like reinforcement theory, it places television within the context of other social agencies.
+ It sees the audience as differentiated by social characteristics, such as age, gender, ethnicity, social class, as well as by their previous media experiences.
− Although it takes account of audiences, it loses sight of the debate about ownership and control over content of the media.
− By concentrating on the pleasures of audiences, it fails to examine the possible differences in cultural capital between groups.

Media, violence and children: a special case?

Before we examine the evidence, there are several points that need to be stated about the definition of violence.

- First, defining the concept of violence is highly complex. Cartoon/fantasy violence does not equate with news footage of real-life violence.
- Operationalising a concept of violence is inevitably difficult. Concepts used by researchers may not be shared or understood by respondents, particularly by children in research studies. Therefore, research that imposes definitions of violence on young audiences is likely to be problematic.
- The broader one's concept of violence is (e.g. verbal abuse, swearing, threats of violence, comic-strip violence, physical and sexual violence), the greater the number of violent acts that will be encountered.
- Violence on television needs to be contextualised in order to understand its meaning and significance. For example, many violent acts on television by 'criminals' are not condoned and the 'baddies' get caught. Therefore, in these programmes these acts are often encoded with messages that crime and violence are not justifiable.

The effects debate was clearly articulated in the well-publicised case of the murder of the toddler James Bulger in 1993 by two young boys. Supposedly, having watched the horror film *Child's Play 3* on video, they acted out some of the atrocities portrayed in the film. There is, however, no incontrovertible evidence that the two boys had actually watched the film.

Popular fears about the effect of televised violence on children

Fear 1: 'TV zombies'

This first fear presupposes that the media are all-powerful, with the corresponding view of the young audience as highly impressionable and vulnerable to media influence. The media are seen as responsible for exploiting the supposedly uncritical child who mindlessly laps up anything seen on the screen. This view of television has also been referred to as the 'plug-in drug' (Winn, 1985).

This view clearly differentiates between what are considered to be desirable and undesirable activities for children. Television is portrayed as an 'evil' that dulls the minds of otherwise inquisitive and lively young people, and brings them into contact with issues, such as sex, which they are considered to be too young to cope with (Postman, 1985).

Fear 2: desensitisation

This fear is based on the assumption that regular viewing of mediated (screen) violence will desensitise the young audience to situational (real-life) violence. As a result of viewing violent acts frequently, they lose their sensitivity to the shock and horror of such violence.

Fear 3: imitation — 'copycat violence'

Children clearly do imitate what they see on television and film. You will undoubtedly have seen young children pretending to be Power Rangers, Turtles or other superheroes, sometimes dressed in outfits like those worn by these fictional characters to make their pretend-play more authentic or convincing. They also imitate the language, skills and narratives of what they see on screen. This imitation is encouraged by some adults as a form of imaginative play and is viewed as a positive stage in child development. However, the fear rests on the assumption that children will also imitate anti-social behaviour.

Challenging the fears

All the previous effect models have been applied to the debate about children and screen violence. They have all been concerned with potential effects. However, today most sociologists of the media would totally reject the notion of the media as all-powerful; it would be far too simplistic to argue that any given media text will affect all members of an audience in the same way. Indeed, most analysts of the media accept the proposition that media texts are read differently by different members of the audience according to their subjective experience, cultural knowledge and their social characteristics. The old debate that focused on television as a 'problem' has been replaced with one which is concerned with the motivations for watching and the pleasures received. Furthermore, Buckingham, Fraser and Maynan (1990) in their work on children and television, found that they had considerably underestimated children's ability to be critical of television.

The mass-culture debate

The Frankfurt School of Marxism

The founders of this school, forced to leave Nazi Germany in the 1930s, fled to America, where they took up a critical position of modern capitalism and mass consumption. They linked modern capitalism with the control exerted by media industries and products over the consumer. Using the concept of 'commodity fetishism', they demonstrated the ways in which cultural forms operate to keep modern capitalism going.

- Commodity fetishism means that the products of people's work become commodities or objects for sale. The products become more valued for their exchange value (the money they can command on the market) than for their use value (their practical use to the consumer). For example, the fact that a particular painting of a bowl of flowers by Van Gogh sold for £23 million tells us much more about the exchange value of the painting than it does about its use value.
- Art and culture were seen as being marketed for profit. Marcuse referred to this mass consumption society as 'one-dimensional' because it generated 'false needs' in the public which could only be met by the culture industry.

- Marcuse et al. argued that the working class has been kept docile and accepting of the status quo by the diet they are fed by the daily media. They focused on popular music, cinema and radio as the means whereby the public audience accepted their situation. They saw popular media forms as ultimately debasing the public and bringing culture down to the lowest common denominator of taste.

Evaluation

- The Frankfurt School position is rather elitist because it assumes that only the founders of the Frankfurt School can distinguish what is worthless and degrading.
- There is no methodology to differentiate between false needs and true needs. For instance, if labour-saving machines allow more leisure time in which we can choose to watch television, go with friends to the cinema etc., in what sense are these false needs?

Key thinkers

Adorno, Marcuse, Horkheimer

Mass media, mass culture, mass society?

Sugrue and Taylor (1996) argue that there are several processes which help to produce a mass culture.
- Culture becomes a product to be consumed, like any other.
- Culture becomes very homogeneous, blurring the boundaries between poor and quality products.
- Technological development produces mass audiences for the mass media.
- Scope for political change, resistance and individual self-identity is diminished.

In general, fears about mass culture and mass society revolve around the loss of authentic and traditional working-class culture, e.g. brass bands, folk dancing, folk festivals and collectivism. Writers like Sugrue and Taylor have paid little attention to any changes in the cultures of the middle, upper-middle or upper classes. Although other writers might see several different positions on the 'mass culture debate', they can be divided more simply into two approaches: pessimistic and optimistic.

Pessimism: the radical and romantic left

- The Frankfurt School saw that the traditional, authentic culture of the working class was under threat from commodity capitalism, which manipulated the masses using a diet of 'bread and circuses'.
- Left-wing literary critics, social historians and cultural theorists such as F. R. Leavis, Richard Hoggart, Raymond Williams and Stuart Hall also mourned the loss of a working-class culture, which they believed to be authentic, vital and spontaneous.

- The romantic left saw education as being the key social institution capable of protecting youth by teaching them how to discriminate between what was 'good' and what was 'bad' in cultural products. Implicit in their arguments was that the products of high culture — opera, classical music and literature — were superior.

More pessimism: the radical right

- Although they share many of the assumptions of the theorists of the Frankfurt School, the radical right's perception of the working class is different.
- For the left, the position of the working class derives from socioeconomic inequality. However, for the radical right there is a 'natural' difference between the elite and the masses.
- This essentially paternalistic view sees the masses as having their own valid, if somewhat simple, rough-hewn culture. Hence nostalgia for 'folk festivals', morris dancing, herbal remedies and story telling — industrialisation and the mass media destroyed this folk-culture and replaced it with low-grade mass culture.

Evaluation

- Pluralists challenge this pessimism and argue that audiences are making active choices.
- Popular culture provides pleasure for audiences.
- Postmodernists would be more optimistic seeing people making choices based on their individual identities, not socioeconomic position.

Deviancy amplification and moral panics

- A moral panic is recognisable by the strength of feeling expressed by a large number of people about a specific group which appears to threaten the social order at a given time.
- Members of this group become the 'folk-devils' about whom 'something needs to be done', i.e. increased social controls which might mean stricter laws, longer sentences, heavier fines, and increased policing of specific areas.

Progress of a moral panic

- A small group commits a deviant act.
- The media report the story and a problem group becomes identified.
- The media search for similar stories, then sensationalise and exaggerate their significance.
- Members of the group become folk-devils and fear of them is encouraged. More deviance occurs as this group is marginalised further.
- Media interest is heightened.

- A moral panic occurs as people become aware of the group as a result of media coverage. Public concern is expressed about ways of dealing with the group. The media and the public call for increased controls by the authorities.
- More social control is introduced. Politicians, police and magistrates respond by invoking harsher measures to stamp down on the deviants. New laws may be introduced.

Characteristics of a moral panic

- **Concern**: there must be awareness that the behaviour of a particular group or category is likely to have negative consequences for the rest of society. This gives rise to public concern.
- **Hostility**: increased hostility is directed at this group, and they become the folk-devils. A clear division opens between 'them', the threateners, and 'us', the threatened.
- **Consensus**: the threat posed by this group to the rest of society is seen as very real. The moral entrepreneurs are vocal and the voices of the opposition are weak and disorganised.
- **Disproportionality**: the reaction to the event is out of proportion to its seriousness. In moral panics, the public is given evidence in statistical form and these figures are often wildly exaggerated.
- **Volatility**: any moral panic has a limited lifetime in the media. It is difficult to sustain a fever pitch of antagonism for any length of time. The public loses interest or the agenda-setters change the focus of their attention.

Deviancy amplification

- Selective reporting by the media can increase deviancy, creating crime waves and social problems.
- The media's attention invokes public concern. People start to ask 'what is to be done about...?' and a social process develops, the outcome of which is likely to be legislative change.
- The use of the concept of 'moral panic' lies within interactionism. However, it can also be placed within a clear hegemonic framework of relations between the state, law and social class.
- The moral panic can be seen as a means of distracting attention from the crises within the capitalist state. Moral panics form part of a legitimising process for identifying 'enemies within' while at the same time strengthening the powers of the state.
- Incidents and phenomena that provoked moral panics analysed by sociologists include: violent conflict between mods and rockers in Britain in the 1960s; mugging; football hooliganism; child sexual abuse; Satanic child abuse; single-parent families; the US drug panic of the late 1980s.

Theories of moral panics

- **The grassroots model**: this model argues that the panic starts with the general public, who become anxious about a specific problem or issue.
- **The elite-engineered model**: elites deliberately and consciously undertake a campaign to create public fear and panic in order to divert attention away from the 'real problems' in society. The mugging panic of the 1970s fits this model.
- **Interest-group theory**: the exercise of power in producing the moral panic comes from middle-level groups, such as professional associations, police departments, media professionals, religious and educational groups. Therefore, in any moral panic we would need to ask the question, 'who benefits?'

Key concepts
moral entrepreneurs; folk devils

Key thinkers
Cohen, Goode and Ben Yehuda, Young, Hall, Kitzinger and Skidmore

Media and ideology

The role of ideology permeates all areas of mass media, including ownership and control of the media, news production, representation, mass culture, politics and the future of the media. The following are brief guidelines to the different positions:

- According to instrumentalist or classical Marxists, the groups that own the means of production also control the dominant ideas of their society. Through ownership of newspapers, television companies and the electronic media, these groups manipulate and dominate the ideas of their audiences.
- News production can be seen as a site of ideological control. Instrumentalists see news as biased in favour of dominant groups, and argue that owners have direct control over news production by controlling editors.
- Hegemonic Marxists argue that ideological control is possible only with the consent of the masses, so media owners have to persuade audiences that the social system is fair and just. This is the outcome of a cultural struggle between competing social, political and ideological forces, and representation is a key site in this struggle. Representation of social groups enables us to see how the process of marginalisation occurs. Groups who are not white, middle-class men are subjected to limited and negative stereotyping. They are seen as 'other' and are therefore marginalised.
- Feminists view the media organisations as patriarchal institutions in which the 'glass ceiling' operates against female professionals. Representations of women, although improving, are still seen as limited and problematic.

- However, pluralists reject the possibility of ideological control. They argue that many different voices are expressed through different media. The audiences are active and can interpret media messages; they choose different media and make sense of the media subjectively. It would, therefore, be impossible for a single group to exert total control over media audiences.
- Postmodernists take a position close to pluralists. As they see a decline in meta-narratives, they deny the possibility of single ideological control.

Questions
&
Answers

This section of the guide provides you with six questions on **Mass Media** in the style of the AQA unit test. These questions examine a variety of aspects of the Mass Media topic and demand a range of examinable skills. The first five questions are followed by a grade-A and a grade-C response. It is important to note that the grade-A answers are not 'model' answers — they do not represent the only, or even necessarily the best, way of answering these questions. It would be quite possible to take a different approach, to use different material, or even to come to a different conclusion, and still gain very high marks. Rather, the answers represent a particular 'style': suitable concepts and studies, displaying a critical and evaluative aware-ness towards the material used, and presenting a logically structured argument. The grade-C answers, meanwhile, are basically on the right track but fail, for various reasons, to score very high marks.

The final question is for you to attempt yourself, with some guidelines to help you with your answer.

Examiner's comments

The candidate answers are accompanied by examiner's comments. These are preceded by the icon 𝑒 and indicate where credit is due. For the grade-A answers, the examiner explains what it is that enables the candidate to score so highly. Particular attention is paid to the candidates' use of the examinable skills: knowledge and under-standing, and identification, analysis, interpretation and evaluation. For the grade-C answers, the examiner points out areas for improvement, specific problems and common errors. You are also invited to rewrite the answer in a way that would gain higher marks, and some pointers are given to show you how you might do this.

Ownership, audiences and ethnic representation

Item A
Pluralist theorists argue that the free market determines the success of media products. Audiences can make or break newspapers, magazines and television programmes. The mass media have to provide audiences with what they want or audiences would cease to buy, listen or watch. Pluralists accept that media content, especially of newspapers, may be biased as it reflects the attitudes of their readership. Bias is a result of audience preferences rather than the influence of media barons or the journalists.

Item B
Some sociologists have focused on the importance of the role of professional managers and editorial staff. It is argued that editors have some independence from owners, but generally the ideas of owners percolate down to editors and are used as a framework within which editors and journalists operate. Other sociologists argue that the news is a result of the way news teams use news values to define what is 'newsworthy' and this is the way that they sell newspapers. However, even if the owners manipulate their editors and journalists, we cannot prove that this affects the audience.

(a) **Explain what is meant by 'media barons' (Item A).** (2 marks)
(b) **Suggest two ways in which media barons may have influence over what appears in the press.** (4 marks)
(c) **Identify three types of audience behaviour influenced by the media.** (6 marks)
(d) **Identify and briefly explain two criticisms of the pluralist view that the audience has the greatest power.** (8 marks)
(e) **Examine the representation of race and ethnicity in the media.** (20 marks)
(f) **With reference to Items A and B and elsewhere, assess the view that ownership of the media is the most important factor in control over media content.** (20 marks)

■ ■ ■

Answer to question 1: grade-C candidate

(a) A media baron is someone like Rupert Murdoch.

question

 There is no definition here, but the candidate has given a correct example. In some circumstances this would score 1 mark, but it is always safer to produce a definition.   **1/2 marks**

(b) Rupert Murdoch sacked an editor of a newspaper because he didn't agree with Murdoch's ideas. Also, some Marxists say that the ideas in the newspaper are those of the owner of that paper.

 The candidate gives two correct examples and scores full marks.   **4/4 marks**

(c) Changing one's attitudes to racism and sexism, becoming violent after watching violent programmes on TV and learning information about people in other countries.

 The candidate has confused attitudes with behaviour here. Only one correct response is given, that of violent behaviour. It is important that you read the question carefully and are clear about what you have to do. The candidate scores only 2 marks.   **2/6 marks**

(d) Marxists argue that the pluralists are wrong because they insist on giving most power to the audience. Marxists say that audiences are passive and manipulated and the only people with power are the owners.

 This is an acceptable criticism, but the question asks for two. The candidate scores 2 + 2 marks, as the criticism is identified and described briefly.   **4/8 marks**

(e) The media are very biased against ethnic minorities and the portrayal is always negative and sees them as troublemakers. An example of this is the article about Benjamin Zephaniah who was going to be the resident poet in one of the top universities. The paper (the *Sun*) said things like 'Would you let your son or daughter be taught by this man?' He is a Rastafarian poet and very well respected, but the newspaper just saw him as someone with dreadlocks who was bound to be trouble.

 The essay starts with a very strong assertion and it may be difficult to move away from this position in the rest of the essay, although the candidate does use a relevant example as illustration.

The advertisements for Benetton clothes made by Toscani have also been accused of being racist. When some students talked to Toscani in a TV programme, he said the only people who were racist were those who saw the images as racist. But he is forgetting that the way we read images is made by our society. He used a photo of two little girls, black and white. The white child was like an angel and the black girl had her hair shaped into horns, but he said that the black girl was the angel and the white one was a devil. This is not what most people would think. I think that this encourages people to be racist.

 Again, the example is relevant to the question, but the candidate is in danger of turning the essay into a list of anecdotal evidence.

Some black and ethnic people are shown as troublemakers like black muggers. A sociologist said that this was not fair and it made people have a lot of concern about black youth on the streets. It was a moral panic.

> The reference here is to Hall et al., but the name needs to be stated and more detailed description is required. Remember that the marks for this essay are weighted heavily towards knowledge and understanding.

So we can see that the portrayal of race and ethnicity is very limited and negative.

> The candidate has been forced to discuss only one viewpoint by taking such an assertive position from the beginning. The essay would have scored more marks if it had used a better structure. More marks could have been gained by making reference to theoretical approaches, too. **10/20 marks**

(f) Ownership of the media since the Second World War has been concentrated in a very few hands. Theories such as instrumentalism, hegemonic Marxism and pluralism have examined the link between ownership and control of the media and produced very different ideas. Golding and Murdock say that allocative control is where the individual has the power to define the overall goals of the organisation and can allocate funding and resources. Operational control is where media professionals carry out the day-to-day running of the organisation. Miliband argued that the state operates in the interests of the ruling class and that the output of the media reflects the dominant ideas of this group. Even entertainment programmes do not challenge the status quo.

> There are some relevant references here, and the candidate differentiates between allocative and operational control.

The strengths of a Marxist theory are that they show that owners hold the power. For example, Harold Evans, then editor of *The Times*, was sacked when he refused to support Murdoch's ideas. However, the weaknesses of the theory are that it sees the audience as passive and easily manipulated. Hegemonic theory focuses on the structures that media professionals work under. It is argued that owners cannot have day-to-day running of media corporations and delegate to professionals who tend to be white, middle-class men with middle-of-the-road political ideas. This is especially clear in the manufacture of news, which involves gatekeeping, agenda-setting and selection based on news values.

> This paragraph shows sound use of supporting evidence in the sacking of Harold Evans. The candidate also demonstrates some understanding of a hegemonic position. There is some evidence of evaluation.

In contrast, the pluralists argue that owners cannot control media output because they can't be in so many different places at once. Pluralists do not accept that a conspiracy exists because many different voices are heard, although they do accept there is bias in the media. They argue that the audience is active, selecting and interpreting media messages, so the owners cannot be in control.

question

 Overall, this is a reasonable essay that is well focused and provides some supporting evidence. However, it lacks a conclusion and does not address the items as the question asks. **13/20 marks**

 The candidate has produced a better response to the final part of the question than to the other parts. This means that the overall mark is of a grade-C standard. **Overall: 34/60**

■ ■ ■

Answer to question 1: grade-A candidate

(a) Media barons are people, usually men, who own large sections of media industries. They are often proprietors of newspapers, such as Rupert Murdoch or Lord Beaverbrook.

 This is a correct response and gives appropriate examples to support the answer. It scores full marks. **2/2 marks**

(b) Media barons can have influence over the press directly, by manipulating their staff and ensuring their views are written up, or indirectly, by influencing editors so that they accept the proprietor's framework of political ideas. They have the power to hire and fire.

 Although these two positions are close, the candidate has differentiated between them by using the terms 'directly' and 'indirectly'. This part of the answer scores full marks. **4/4 marks**

(c) There are different ways that audience behaviour is affected: watching violence on screen may increase aggression, consumption is increased after watching advertisements, and imitation may occur. Some people say that copycat violence occurs after riots are shown on television.

 The candidate gives three reasons and does not fall into the trap of referring to audience effects unrelated to behaviour. **6/6 marks**

(d) Pluralists do not accept that even when audiences make choices, those very choices are limited by the concentration of ownership of media products, so they are choosing between similar products owned by very large companies. Although pluralists rightly point out that audiences can switch off their televisions or not buy certain papers, that is really the only power they have. They do not make the news because news values are usually about celebrities. The only time ordinary people make news is when they are involved in disasters. News comes from official sources, not ordinary people.

 This is a good response, but it would be clearer if the candidate had introduced the two criticisms with subheadings and then explained them more fully. This makes it easier for examiners to award the correct marks. The candidate again scores full marks. Try to think of other criticisms of the pluralist position here.

8/8 marks

(e) Many sociologists have examined the representation of race and ethnicity in the media and most of them have shown that it has been mainly negative and limited until recently. We can answer this question by using the framework given by Alvarado et al. who showed that these representations fall into four main categories: the dangerous, the exotic, the pitied and the humorous.

🖉 This is a clear start which lays down the areas that the essay will expand upon.

We could argue that the 'dangerous' category is the most important because hegemonic Marxist sociologists such as Hall argue that the audience is affected by the limited stereotyping of ethnic groups by the media. In this category we can find the portrayal of muggers as young, black men who seemed to have been singled out for negative treatment by the metropolitan police. The image of muggers and mugging led to a moral panic over street crime. Black youths have also been closely associated with drugs and other forms of criminality. For example, 'Gangsta Rap' has been given a bad press because of the crimes of Puff Daddy and members of the So Solid Crew. Van Djik also showed that in the newspapers race was portrayed very negatively.

🖉 It is very useful to take a framework like Alvarado's for this essay because it helps to hang the evidence on to specified 'hooks'. The candidate is using the material very well and it is clear there is some relevant sociological research evidence to call upon.

Most of this research is now quite out of date, but the recent representations of Muslims and asylum-seekers can be seen to be a continuation of ethnicity as a dangerous category. We might say that the portrayal of asylum-seekers has been the latest moral panic, and press reporting of items relating to Muslims since 11 September has been almost wholly negative. This is called 'Islamophobia'.

🖉 Here the candidate introduces some evaluation and analysis. It is important to be aware that some research evidence can be rather dated and you will always be rewarded for relevant contemporary material used sociologically.

Representation of black people as the pitied is mainly in relation to famines and other disasters. We see images of starving children on posters for charities helping developing countries, and the latest news coming out of Africa focuses on AIDS victims — often children. This may encourage ethnocentric attitudes to black Africa.

Exotic images are still found on television. Adverts for travel to foreign countries often show the people dressed in national costume and refer to places as 'magical' and 'mystical'. Again, this can encourage ethnocentric attitudes. Some adverts, especially for the Caribbean (like Lilt ads), portray images of laziness and lack of 'Western' work attitudes.

The humorous category may not be so relevant today. Programmes like *Mind Your Language, Love Thy Neighbour* and *It Ain't Half Hot Mum* can be seen as extremely racist. However, organisations like the Campaign Against Racism in the Media (CARM) actively campaigned to stop such racism on television. Films like *Tarzan* are now seen as dated, but some people might think that the Indiana Jones films were racist.

> These are sound examples and although they are not exactly sociological research, they have been used to advantage by the candidate.

Theorists have different views as to why these images are like this. The instrumentalist Marxists might see it as a means of dividing the working class, to prevent them from becoming united. While we can see asylum-seekers as trouble for the country, we are less likely to appreciate the conditions that led them to seek asylum in the first place. Hegemonic Marxists would see these images as part of the process of marginalisation. These groups are shown as 'not like us' and so we feel that we are the 'respectables' and our consent is won over for the status quo. Pluralists would disagree considerably. They would say that the images of race and ethnicity are simply reflections of the contemporary society and as such they are not static. As members of ethnic minorities become more accepted in Britain, so their portrayal changes. They would use the example that the most trusted person in Britain in 2002 was Trevor Macdonald.

> By ending the essay with a variety of perspectives the candidate demonstrates a sound grasp of the subject. It is not necessary to wait until the last section of the essay to do this, but in order to gain as many marks as possible, always try to include the theoretical explanations. This essay has a sound framework, relevant research evidence and contemporary examples, and contains some analysis and evaluation. **18/20 marks**

(f) There are three main theoretical positions involved in this argument. They are the instrumentalist Marxist, hegemonic Marxist and pluralist approaches. Item B says that the ideas of the owners percolate down to editors and are used as a framework. This instrumentalist position sees the media owners as a rich and powerful group who benefit considerably from capitalism and who therefore have a special interest in ensuring its survival. They manipulate media output directly so that it reflects their own interests and so maintains their powerful position. These Marxists go as far as to suggest that the editors have little power and simply carry out what the owners want.

> This is a very clear and coherent introduction. The candidate has a sound grasp of the instrumentalist view and reference is made to Item B.

Owners share similar backgrounds and therefore interests. As members of the privileged ruling group they run their industries according to their own best interests.

Murdoch owns and controls News Corporation, a multimedia corporation with global interests which in the UK include the *Sun, News of the World, The Times* and *Sunday Times* as well as BSkyB and Fox. When Sky Broadcasting bid for coverage of Manchester United Football Club, all the press except the *Sun* and *The Times* condemned the move. This clearly supports the statement that ownership equates with control.

🖉 There is useful supporting evidence here. As this essay is weighted towards AO2 skills, you must be aware that you need to identify and interpret evidence in your work.

However, there are criticisms of this perspective. Pluralists argue that people hold widely differing views, not just a single, dominant one. It is physically impossible for owners to be involved in the day-to-day running of such diverse media empires. Owners are controlled too; they are governed by a number of regulations such as the Official Secrets Act and laws of libel, and are monitored by the Press Complaints Commission.

🖉 There is explicit evaluation here which draws usefully on a contrasting perspective. Analysis is evident in the way that the candidate develops the argument.

Hegemonic Marxists take a similar position to instrumentalists in the sense that they believe that the media produce ideologically biased material, but they do not agree that the media corporations are under direct control of the owners. They say that it is physically impossible for a media baron to be in different parts of the world at the same time. Media professionals have control over the day-to-day running of the corporations. These people have been socialised into the ideas of providing commercially successful media products and they control the output of the media. As they are a privileged group in themselves — white, middle-class men, sharing a similar view of the world — the media messages that they produce reflect their own positions. For example, as Item B says, they use news values to define what is newsworthy.

🖉 The candidate has clearly grasped the fundamentals of the hegemonic position. Many students find this approach challenging and it is worth making sure that you can explain the differences between the instrumentalist and hegemonic Marxist positions.

Media professionals help in the process of winning the consent of the majority by marginalising the groups seen as potential threats to that consensus. Although they take a Marxist position, seeing media as supporting the interests of capitalism, they do not view audiences as passive. The ruling groups engage in a 'cultural struggle', allowing some concessions to keep the majority with them.

🖉 This is sound analysis and shows further evidence of AO2 skills.

Taking a completely different approach are the pluralists. They argue that the media do not speak with one voice, nor does one group hold power at the expense

question

of all others. Even though there is concentration of ownership, modern society is democratic and can operate freedom of choice. There are challenging and alternative voices in the media, but people may not wish to listen. The media are in the business of giving the public what it wants, otherwise the media industries would collapse. Pluralists maintain that governments constrain the power of media bosses, and in the USA, the huge film studios have on more than one occasion been prevented from owning film production, distribution and cinemas at the same time. Journalists and editors often refuse to accept owners' desires and investigative journalism has often targeted the powerful.

In evaluating these approaches, the instrumental Marxists support the statement, but their view appears to be overly simplistic. It fails to take into account the potential power of active audiences in making their demands known. However, in accepting the power of audiences the pluralists fail to address where the audiences get their ideas from in the first place.

This is an impressive essay and with a stronger conclusion could gain 20/20 marks. Always try to find time to conclude your essay satisfactorily, in a way that proceeds naturally from the structure of your argument. **19/20 marks**

Overall, this candidate has produced an excellent set of responses to the question. The answers demonstrate effective knowledge and understanding as well as strong analytical and evaluative skills. They also make very good use of supporting evidence. **Overall: 57/60**

News production, ideology and gender representation

Item A

Newsgathering is a highly selective process. Interactionists argue that although many thousands of potential news events take place every day, as a result of selection processes only very few get broadcast or printed. Gatekeeping and agenda-setting are crucial in understanding the construction of our news.

Item B

Pluralists believe that the mass media reflect the role of women in society and that the images of women change as the role of women changes. The newer representations of women reflect their enhanced role in the economic sphere and their increased independence. Increasingly, media professionals are female and many strong female characters appear in soaps and police dramas. In this way representations of women and of men are fair reflections of gender roles in society as a whole.

(a) Explain what is meant by the term 'gatekeeping' (Item A).   (2 marks)
(b) Identify two groups of people who can act as gatekeepers in the news
    production process.   (4 marks)
(c) Suggest three ways in which the news may be biased.   (6 marks)
(d) Identify and explain two feminist criticisms of media institutions.   (8 marks)
(e) Examine the view that the media are inevitably ideological.   (20 marks)
(f) Using the material in Item B and elsewhere, assess the view that the
    representation of gender in the media is an accurate reflection of gender
    roles in modern society.   (20 marks)

■ ■ ■

Answer to question 2: grade-C candidate

(a) Gatekeeping means that some potential news is stopped by editors from being published, whilst other stories are allowed through.

   🖉 The candidate defines the concept correctly and is awarded 2 marks. **2/2 marks**

(b) Editors and readers.

   🖉 The candidate scores 2 marks for editors, but nothing for readers.   **2/4 marks**

question

(c) Marxists say that one way the news can be biased is that managers and bosses are shown in a more favourable light than workers are and we are expected to take the side of the bosses against the workers. Another example of bias is that in wartime the enemy is always shown badly. The language of the Gulf War coverage showed this when 'our boys' were heroes and theirs were not. Galtung and Ruge say that most of the news is about elite people, e.g. in the Bali bombing we only heard about the deaths of Australian and British people. It seems as though the Indonesians didn't matter. This is another kind of bias.

 There are three correct examples here and the candidate scores full marks.

6/6 marks

(d) Women are shown as sex symbols or domestics. For example, Tuchman argued that women were symbolically annihilated and this has not changed.

 The candidate has misunderstood the question and assumes the issue is about representation and not media institutions. Unfortunately, no marks can be awarded for this part of the question.

0/8 marks

(e) When used by Marxists, the term 'ideology' means that the dominant ideas in society are those of the ruling class. Instrumental Marxists would say that the media are definitely ideological and that the media are biased towards some groups like white, middle-class men. Althusser said that the media industry is an ideological state apparatus and it is used by the ruling class to maintain the status quo. This means that other groups don't get a fair deal and what we get in the media is one-sided. Other sociologists, mainly the pluralists, say that the media actually show different sides and individuals can make up their minds what they want to watch and read and what they remember about it.

 This is a sound introduction. It states the hegemonic view and compares it with a pluralist approach. There is an attempt to define 'ideological', which is always useful in an essay of this kind.

We can see that someone like Rupert Murdoch who owns a lot of the media would want to keep his position so his newspapers would not publish anything about the ruling class that showed them in a bad light. Some Marxists would say that because he owns a lot of media he must also control what comes out of the media. For example, he backed Blair in the last two elections even though he had backed Thatcher before. This shows he wants to be on the winning side and keep selling his papers.

 There is some evidence here but the style is relatively simplistic. The statement about Blair needs to be developed.

In wartime, the media are biased because they are always on the side of 'our boys'. The GMG has studied several wars and argues that war news is always ideological. Since 11 September there has been a lot of news about Muslims and it is much more negative than positive. Some people in Britain might think that all

Muslims are problems and I know this isn't right because our town has lots of different kinds of people and they get on all right together.

🖉 The candidate is applying contemporary events sociologically and there is a hint of evaluation here.

Another way the media are biased is against black youth. Stuart Hall said that mugging was made up just to turn people's attention to blacks so they wouldn't think about the crisis of capitalism. This is a moral panic and it usually brings changes in the law even if there hasn't really been much happening. There has been bias against other young groups too, like the mods and rockers. Eileen Barker said that the media represented Moonies as brainwashing people. So we can see that the media do not always give everybody a fair chance. Some groups like the rich are all right, but others get ideological bias.

🖉 Again, there is some rather unsophisticated knowledge and understanding, but it is applied appropriately. The concluding sentence mainly repeats what has already been said. Think how you might rewrite this essay to improve it. **13/20 marks**

(f) Item B is about the pluralist position on gender representation. Pluralists do not usually take a very critical position like the feminists do, but say that things are gradually getting better and will improve even more as women's lives change. The problem with this is 'How long do we have to wait?' They assume that it will be all right in the end, but if people don't take a stand things won't change.

🖉 This is a reasonable introduction. The candidate has correctly interpreted the item, but the last two sentences are verging on the obvious. This should be avoided in a sociological essay.

The mass media have always been biased in their view of gender. We only have to look at page 3 in the *Sun* to see that this is the case. A topless woman or girl may be pleasing to some people but we are supposed to live in an age of equality and not discrimination. This kind of stereotyping is created by patriarchal society. One sociologist found that only 6% of management in the media were women and this is clearly the case now.

🖉 The candidate is losing focus on the question set and has not yet addressed the issue of representation.

Naomi Wolf criticised this negative portrayal of women in *The Beauty Myth*. She said that to see a woman in a magazine or paper in a sexual pose gave men the idea that all women were simply sex objects. There is also a problem for young women who are shown very thin models and told that 'thin is in'. In magazines for girls they may have articles about eating disorders but their models are all very thin. Images of men have changed too and men's magazines are very popular and show images of beautiful, well-toned bodies. Some young men are getting eating disorders as well. There has also been a complaint to the advertisers that too many show men as puny and downtrodden and show women as more powerful. So the

pluralists may be right here, as some women are being shown as stronger. There are several women in the main roles in police dramas like *Prime Suspect, Silent Witness* and *Mersey Beat*.

> There is a useful reference to Naomi Wolf and to the construction of body image. Some recognition is made of changes in representation. The candidate does not conclude the essay. **10/20 marks**

> **Overall, the candidate needs to have a more secure knowledge and understanding. The essays need to be more focused.** **Overall: 33/60**

■ ■ ■

Answer to question 2: grade-A candidate

(a) Gatekeeping refers to the ways in which editors are able to allow some information into news bulletins and prevent other information from being made public.

> This is a good response. The candidate gains full marks. **2/2 marks**

(b) Editors and politicians.

> These two are correct and the candidate gains 2 marks for each. Think which other groups would be relevant here. **4/4 marks**

(c) Examples of bias in the news may occur in wartime when the government issues 'D notices' stopping information being published, especially if it shows the government in a bad light. Agenda-setting means that certain topics are focused on at the expense of others and these are likely to be in favour of some groups rather than others. Marxists would argue that the news is ideological because the truth of real oppression of the workers is never shown.

> The candidate has given three valid suggestions of bias (D notices, agenda-setting and hiding the truth of oppression), plus some interesting though not essential elaboration. **6/6 marks**

(d) First, feminists would argue that media institutions are essentially patriarchal and that although there are more women's faces on television, they have hardly made any impact on the hierarchy of the media organisations. Second, radical feminists would argue that the content of media products is degrading and harmful to women. The pornography industry is financially successful by exploiting women and benefiting men.

> This is a sound answer. Both points are valid and each is identified and explained briefly. The answer scores 2 + 2 marks for each point **8/8 marks**

(e) Marxists believe that the media are inevitably ideological. This means that the media represent the interests of the powerful in society. Writers such as Miliband and Althusser saw the media as a powerful, legitimating force for the ruling class.

Miliband referred to the media as the 'new opium of the people' since they distorted the true nature of oppression and exploitation in society and, like religion, offered a kind of diversion for the masses. Althusser stressed that the media were simply another ideological state apparatus brainwashing the working class into a state of false consciousness.

🖉 In an excellent introduction, the candidate shows a good grasp of the classical Marxist approach and an ability to develop an argument coherently.

However, hegemonic Marxists see the relationship between the media and class conflict as more complex. They reject a conspiracy explanation and argue that although the media present a narrow worldview, the majority of people come to accept this view as natural and normal because they have been won over. We can see this with the large number of people who watch programmes such as *Who Wants to be a Millionaire?* and *Big Brother*. Hegemonic Marxists such as the GMG have shown that the news is very biased and reporting of strikes and the Gulf War tended to be one-sided.

🖉 Good, explicit evaluation is present here. The candidate demonstrates a sound grasp of hegemonic theory and makes use of appropriate examples as evidence.

From another perspective, feminists also see the media as ideological but this time in terms of gender. They argue that the media operate within a patriarchal society and reflect the dominant interests of men. Early content analyses based on gender showed that women appeared less often on television and in limited roles. Tuchman argued that the media symbolically annihilated women.

🖉 Here the candidate makes very pleasing use of feminism as a critique, which many students might have failed to do. It is easy to concentrate on Marxism and pluralism and ignore the feminist criticisms.

Another way in which the media are said to be ideological is through the representation of both ethnicity and disability. Alvarado's work showed that ethnic minorities were represented in very limited categories. He named them the exotic, the dangerous, the humorous and the pitied. Tom Shakespeare's work demonstrates that representations of disability have tended to reinforce the view that disabled people are evil, courageous or superhuman so that disability is a deviant characteristic.

🖉 Strong supporting evidence is used on ethnicity and disability. This would be rewarded by the examiner.

In contrast, pluralists argue that although the media are biased, it is not necessarily a conscious process. In terms of representation they argue that media images change as society changes. They would also argue that even if there is ideological bias, the most important group is the audience which is active and can see through such bias.

📝 Explicit evaluation is combined in this paragraph with a pleasing use of the pluralist approach. However, the candidate does not conclude the essay.   **17/20 marks**

(f) The portrayal of gender by the media is not an accurate representation of gender roles in modern society. This is more the case with women. Item B makes reference to the pluralist position which says that women's roles change as women's position changes in society. However, the research does not seem to support this viewpoint and much of the early feminist content analyses showed that women were portrayed in limited ways.

📝 The candidate has decided to take an explicitly evaluative position from the beginning of this essay. Although this is quite unusual, it can be highly rewarded. Reference is made to the item too. It is a good idea to do this as soon as you can (when the question asks you to). It is easy to forget to do so later on.

One of the stereotypical images is the way women are shown in magazines. Studies by Ferguson and McRobbie emphasised the way women are 'looked at'. Ferguson called it the 'cult of femininity' and McRobbie demonstrated the way that romance was prioritised in articles and stories for girls and women. The study *Forever Feminine* also showed the way women were supposed to concentrate on their appearance in order to find a boyfriend or husband.

📝 Good supporting evidence is used well. Be aware, though, that this material is now quite dated.

However, a later study showed that magazines were paying more attention to women and careers. Despite this, the view still exists that love, sex, marriage and partnership remain important features of women's lives. The ideology of femininity remains strong. Daily newspapers still stereotype women in relation to men and to their physical characteristics such as 'blonde wife of politician X'.

📝 The candidate is aware that changes have taken place. There is a strong evaluative tone here.

Men have traditionally been accorded more respect and a wider variety of representations. However, this has changed over the last decade. Men's bodies are now displayed in similar ways to those of women. There is more homoerotic photography, due to the introduction of men's magazines such as *GQ* and *FHM*. These magazines deliberately widened their readership to include gay audiences with consumer power. Magazines like *Loaded* have emphasised the younger man as a 'lad' interested only in football, beer and sex.

📝 Many candidates fall into the trap of only examining women's representation in an essay on gender. This candidate, however, is aware of male representation and also refers to gay men as consumers.

Several studies have counted the numbers of appearances, locations and work roles of men and women in television advertisements. Work by Cumberbatch documents the differences between the use of males and females in adverts. Women stereo-typically advertise household and beauty products while men still appear in motoring and financial product advertising. Voice-overs are traditionally male unless for beauty products, and the voice of authority remains male for most advertising. Rosalind Coward talks of the female body as 'work in progress'.

ℤ The candidate uses appropriate studies and widens the evidence to cover television advertising.

In video games, women are represented as stereotypically pneumatic — either as heroines like Lara Croft or (more typically, according to a study called *Video Kids*) as characters needing to be rescued. Even in music videos, women are under-represented. They are typically shown as passive and submissive, but these are the results of the researcher's own constructs in analysing them. Vincent et al. said that sexism was a major part of music videos.

One of the more recent concerns for researchers in terms of gender represen-tation is body image. There appears to be a body fascism operating in the media, especially for women. Men can still appear in many different shapes and degrees of attractiveness, but women are commented upon if they do not conform to stereotypical expectations of size and attractiveness. Several young women in popular culture suffer from eating disorders, like Calista Flockhart, Geri Halliwell and many 'superwaif' models. Some commentators have argued that this has an adverse effect on girls who may be persuaded to believe that they need to be thin to be acceptable.

ℤ This is very impressive. The candidate has clearly revised a wide range of media sources and puts them to effective use in this answer.

In conclusion we can see that the media create ideal and idealised images of men and women. Although there has been some change, there is still a cultural lag between what's happening in society and what's happening in the media.

ℤ It is refreshing to see a conclusion that is evaluative and does not simply restate what has already been said. This is an excellent response to the question and the candidate deserves full marks. **20/20 marks**

ℤ **This candidate is well aware of the essential skills and has produced a set of excellent responses.** **Overall: 57/60**

News construction, representation and effects

Item A

In news reports, representations of Asian youth tend to focus on 'Asian gangs' and religious extremism, either through Islamic movements or Hindu nationalism. It is equally clear from recent reports that there are small sections of the British Asian population which are involved in extreme nationalistic movements. These issues of moral concern exist alongside fears of Asian criminality and gang formation and echo wider domestic disquiet over the settlement of postwar immigrants.

Source: Les Back (2002) 'Youth, "race" and violent disorder', *Sociology Review*, Vol. 11, No. 4.

Item B

When consulting media sources about such cases as the death of Damilola Taylor, you should be aware of news values — certain criteria and techniques employed by media producers to arouse the interest of readers and thereby sell more news. The danger is that they may distort your impression of the world. It may seem to you that murders of certain types of people, such as children, are common or increasing rapidly, but it is unlikely to be true. The very fact that an event is only regarded as news if it is unexpected and unusually shocking should make you wary of alarmist headlines.

Source: Jill Swale (2001) 'Crime in the news: the Damilola Taylor case', *Sociology Review*, Vol. 11, No. 1.

(a) Explain what is meant by 'representations' (Item A). (2 marks)

(b) Identify two criteria which help to make an event newsworthy. (4 marks)

(c) Suggest three ways in which ethnic minority groups have been represented negatively by the media. (6 marks)

(d) Identify and briefly explain two media effects on audience behaviour. (8 marks)

(e) Examine the 'hypodermic syringe' and 'two-step flow' models of audience effects. (20 marks)

(f) With reference to the items and elsewhere, assess the view that the news is socially constructed. (20 marks)

■ ■ ■

Answer to question 3: grade-C candidate

(a) Representations are the images of certain groups in the media like women shown as housewives in the kitchen.

> ✎ The candidate understands the concept and gives an example to illustrate it. This scores 2 marks. It is useful to add an example as it confirms that you understand the concept. **2/2 marks**

(b) Negativity = bad news.

> ✎ Although the candidate only gives one brief criterion, it is acceptable. Another criterion is required for full marks. **2/4 marks**

(c) As sportspeople, muggers and pop stars.

> ✎ Only one of these (muggers) is correct. The candidate did not read the question carefully enough. **2/6 marks**

(d) Violence — some people believe that watching violence on TV or film will make the audience violent. This was shown in the case of Nathan Martinez in America. He watched *Natural Born Killers* 11 times and then killed his stepmother and sister.

> ✎ The point made is acceptable but only one effect is identified and explained. The answer scores 2 + 2 marks. **4/8 marks**

(e) The hypodermic syringe model of the audience is just what it says. It means that the media are a drug and that they are injected into the blood stream of the audience. The media have a very powerful effect like heroin on individuals and can change their behaviour in very violent ways. This was shown in Bandura's study of children and the Bobo doll. He said that children imitate what they see on television. We have sadly seen this in the case of James Bulger where the two boys watched a film and kidnapped and killed him. However, not all sociologists agree that the audience is so passive and affected by the media in this way.

> ✎ The candidate has some understanding of the hypodermic syringe model and has made reference to Bandura's work.

The two-step flow model is one of the earliest models of media effects. It says that opinion leaders spread media messages to other people and they are active and the rest are not.

Since this model there have been many others and they all deal with the active audience. Uses and gratifications looked at the ways people used the media to meet their needs. There were four different kinds of needs — diversion, surveillance, relationships and one other, so if you wanted information, you would read a newspaper or watch the news. There is also a personal relationship that you can make with people in the media and this helps people who are lonely and so they identify with some of the characters in soaps.

 It seems that this candidate has little to say about the models referred to in the question, and has resorted to looking at others that are more familiar.

The next model is cultivation analysis. This is the dripping tap model that says that if you spend a lot of time with the media you will end up believing what you see. People who only read the *Sun* will believe that women are only sex objects because that is how they are shown. Gerbner said that if you watched a lot of television you would believe that the world is full of criminals and is 'mean'. People who are able to get out in the world do not think that this is the case.

 The candidate has a grasp of the various models in this area, but they are presented in a relatively unsophisticated way and are not used as points of comparison with the models in the question.

The final model is where the audience is really active and the media don't make any difference at all. Marxists say that we are all manipulated by the media so that all these models must be wrong.

 There is evidence that the candidate has an awareness of the more recent work (e.g. the reference to Marxist theory in the last sentence), but again it is limited. Insufficient attention is paid to the question, and overall the essay indicates that the candidate has failed to revise all of the media effects models thoroughly and has therefore used material that isn't directly relevant. The essay lacks evaluation and there is little development of ideas. **10/20 marks**

(f) I think that what we hear about or read in the news is socially constructed. We don't always hear the full or true story, but what journalists think makes a good story. There are many things that determine what we get as news. Marxists say that the ruling class are at the top of society and want to stay that way so the media would not present any news that challenges them. Gatekeepers, like editors, act to allow some news of the ruling class through and stop others. That is why we sometimes hear scandals about the royals, but a lot of the time, Official Secrets Acts and libel law prevent us from being told things.

 Although the candidate has referred to a Marxist analysis of the news, there is no explicit demonstration that the concept of social construction has been understood. Remember that the examiner will be looking to reward explicit knowledge and understanding.

In Item B it says that a case like a murder of a child makes the news because it is very shocking, and because we are told the story over a long time it makes us believe there must be lots of cases like this. It can become a moral panic as people get more worried about violence done by children.

 By making reference to the concept of the moral panic the candidate uses the item to show implicitly that news is socially constructed.

However, the news will not become news if it is not 'newsworthy'. This means that journalists and broadcasters decide what is more newsworthy than something else. Two sociologists did research on newspapers and found a set of criteria they called news values which were a kind of filter for events to become news. The Damilola case was news because it fitted into these news values. It was negative, a murder, and unexpected because it was children murdering a child. It was culturally relevant because it took place in London. All these aspects made it a national news item.

This is a very good paragraph. The candidate uses, interprets and analyses the item and applies it to the concept of news values. It would be useful to refer to Galtung and Ruge by name.

Some sociologists say that because the news is written about by white, middle-class men it reflects the way they see the world. This is a hegemonic position and again shows that news is constructed, not just a set of true facts. They also say that journalists learn how to select some news items instead of others. This is agenda-setting and it is the way that any newspaper or television news is made and the running order of the news. We get a set of ideas about the world from the news as it tells us who and what are important. Obviously, there are going to be inaccuracies and bias in the news. Even when photojournalists select photographs for the news, they put them together to tell a particular story.

In this coherent paragraph the candidate maintains the focus on the question.

However, the pluralists say there is not one bias but many and so it doesn't really matter. They say that audiences are active and if we don't like a particular paper we can buy another — we don't have to buy the *Sun*. In conclusion, people who work for newspapers and TV newsrooms socially construct the news. Marxists say that this works in the interests of the ruling class but the pluralists disagree and say that audiences are more powerful.

The candidate is rewarded for producing a conclusion. Overall, this is a well-focused essay that makes reference to the items and demonstrates sound AO2 skills. **15/20 marks**

Although the candidate did not score highly in the short-answer questions, there is one good essay and this helps to give a good overall mark.
Overall: 35/60

■ ■ ■

Answer to question 3: grade-A candidate

(a) Representation is the process by which certain images come to be processed by the media. These images of groups, events, countries etc. are representations.

This is a good response and the candidate scores full marks. **2/2 marks**

(b) Galtung and Ruge demonstrated the criteria of news values which events have to meet to become news items. Two of these are references to elite people and countries and McLurg's Law.

> This is a clear response and gains full marks. It would be a good idea to learn the list of news values as they are useful for short questions like this as well as for essays on news construction and ideology. **4/4 marks**

(c) Alvarado et al. argued that ethnic minorities have been shown in limited and stereotypical ways by the media. These are 'humorous, dangerous, pitied and exotic'.

> The candidate locates these representations in a correct sociological research framework and gains full marks. **6/6 marks**

(d) Two kinds of media effects on behaviour are: reinforcing and encouraging consumption patterns, and the encouragement of aggression through watching television violence. Marxists argue that by constantly showing us adverts and lifestyle programmes we learn 'false needs' so we buy things we don't really need. Some researchers like William Belson have shown that boys become more aggressive if they have watched a lot of violence on television when they are young.

> Two effects are identified and explained clearly. They are also referenced. **8/8 marks**

(e) The two-step flow model was created by Katz and Lazarsfeld in 1955. It was an important model because it changed the way researchers looked at media effects. Up until this time many researchers had adopted the direct effects or hypodermic syringe model which said that the media worked like a needle injecting messages into the audience. Although this model still has credibility with some people, especially moral entrepreneurs, the importance of the new model was that it changed ideas from being media-centric to the idea that there were relationships within the audience that affected the interpretation of media messages.

> This very good introductory paragraph identifies Katz and Lazarsfeld's work and locates the models chronologically.

The two-step flow model started during the 1940s, with political campaigns in the USA. Lazarsfeld and other researchers interviewed people about their ideas before and after the political campaigns. They discovered that rather than everyone being directly affected by political messages to the same extent, some people were better informed than others and they influenced these other people to change their ideas. The researchers said this showed that the audience is not a mass of people being manipulated: people's relationships with others affect the way they get to understand the media. The model was called a two-step flow model because the media message went from the media source (e.g. radio) to particular people who were especially interested and from them on to the rest of the audience. The interested people were called opinion leaders.

✍ The candidate demonstrates good knowledge and understanding of the two-step flow model.

We may find this a rather out-of-date idea today because researchers like reception analysts tell us that everyone in the audience is actively deconstructing and interpreting media messages and even children learn to become media literate when they are still very young.

The strengths of the two-step flow model are that it was the first to take away the power of direct effects assumed by the hypodermic syringe model and it looked at media within social relationships. Uses and gratifications theorists took this idea further. They said that audiences were active and had needs that they wanted to be gratified by the media. However, there are still people who believe in the direct effects of media on audiences. Instrumentalist Marxists, for instance, say that audiences are passive and manipulated. The Frankfurt School of Marxists say that we are fed a diet of bread and circuses and we learn to put up with it, so we accept mass culture as if it is what we really wanted.

The main weaknesses of the two-step flow model are that it does not explain why there are only two steps and not more, and that we don't know how to predict who will be an opinion leader at any time. We may all be opinion leaders for different people on different subjects at different times, so this does not make it a very strong model to use.

✍ Even though the marks for the question are weighted towards AO1 skills, there is a strong evaluative tone here. The candidate deals with strengths and weaknesses of the models but in an imbalanced manner and doesn't conclude the essay.

15/20 marks

(f) Many people see news as facts simply transmitted onto television screens or printed in newspapers. But this is incorrect as sociological evidence shows that it is nearly impossible for news to be objective and there are all sorts of processes involved in making events into news. According to Item B, news stories like Damilola Taylor's murder are subject to a set of news values. Cases like this are so shocking that they get a lot of media coverage, which makes us think that they are part of a trend.

✍ This is a good, evaluative introduction. The candidate makes reference to the item and applies it well to the question.

Hegemonic Marxists see the news as socially constructed according to different news-making processes and therefore as subjective. One way that news is constructed or manufactured is the idea of gatekeeping. This is simply how an event becomes a news item. Each event has to pass a series of metaphorical gates before it can be called news and is transmitted by the media. The people controlling the process are called gatekeepers and they are usually editors, journalists or news sources. Clearly, this process is subjective.

✎ Here the candidate shows a clear understanding of gatekeeping as one aspect of social construction of the news.

D. M. White researched this process and found that a person's political orientation had an effect, even if minor, of biasing news selection. So gatekeeping is relevant for the title here.

Another part of the process is the role of primary definers, who occupy a privileged position in what Hall calls a hierarchy of access to the media. Primary definers may be first on the scene but are often spokespeople for authoritative sources. This over-accessing can lead to bias, as research by the GMG has shown. A primary definer can shape the news story and hence the views that audiences hold.

✎ The candidate has a sound grasp of hegemonic theory and explains and develops the concept of the primary definer well.

Hegemonic Marxists would see this as promoting the interests of the powerful and not damaging the dominant ideology. Primary definers can be unreliable, as the GMG has shown in relation to coverage of the Falklands War. (However, the GMG is itself influenced by theoretical positions and is therefore not objective.)

News values are criteria that act as a filtering process for news creation. Galtung and Ruge researched the process and discovered that stories have to comply with these criteria to be included. There are both practical and social factors affecting the process. Practical ones include space available, other competing stories and deadlines. Social factors include negativity, cultural relevance, reference to elites and elite nations etc. Negativity is the idea that bad news is good news — stories of crimes, disasters and scandal are usually newsworthy. Cultural relevance refers to McLurg's Law — one Brit is more newsworthy than many more from other nations. The criterion of elites and elite nations means that a story about, say, the US president will generally be included.

✎ The argument is developed well. The candidate has a clear grasp of news values.

As we have seen, the news-making process involves many different factors. Instrumentalist Marxists would say that the news is generated to support bourgeois ideology, and legitimates the powerful. They see a deliberate manipulation of audiences into false consciousness. However, hegemonic Marxists see it not as a conspiracy but as a result of the day-to-day running of newsrooms. They argue that inferential structures create patterns of news. Media professionals are socialised into news-making and learn what makes for commercially successful news bulletins and what sells papers. They are white, middle-class males with a consensual view of the world; this influences their selection of news items and the news is the result.

However, pluralists disagree with the Marxist approach. They do not accept the idea of a dominant ideology, but argue that the media speak with many voices. There is no systematic bias favouring a single group.

✎ Good AO2 skills are apparent here.

In conclusion, there is a great deal of sociological evidence to show that the news is created from highly subjective processes. News cannot be impartial as it is always from a particular position — whether that of government or of groups challenging them. Pluralists see no systematic bias in the news process and argue that audiences have choice over which newspaper to read and which television channel to watch.

🗨 This is an excellent, well-focused essay that demonstrates very good knowledge and understanding together with a strong evaluative tone. **18/20 marks**

🗨 **Overall, the candidate secures full marks for the first four parts and this provides a sound basis for the total score. The essays are both well-focused and demonstrate all the necessary skills.** **Overall: 53/60**

Moral panics, audiences and news production

Item A

A moral panic can be recognised in the intensity of feeling expressed by a large number of people about a particular group of people who appear to threaten the status quo at a particular time. These people become the 'folk devils', and 'moral entrepreneurs' demand that something is done about them. This 'something' usually takes the form of increased social control, which might mean stricter laws, longer sentences, heavier fines and increased policing. After these new controls the panic subsides until a new one emerges.

Adapted from Marsha Jones and Emma Jones (1999) *Mass Media*, Macmillan.

Item B

The work of some researchers, notably the Centre for Contemporary Cultural Studies, emphasised the importance of audience pleasures and highlighted people's creative abilities to reinterpret mainstream texts for their own (subversive) ends. It also highlighted the factors outside the media (such as social class position) which influenced how people made sense of media messages. However, since then a great deal of audience reception research has focused on the diversity of audience interpretations as if this were evidence of straightforward audience 'freedom'. Indeed, audience reception research now emphasises that audiences are not passive recipients of predetermined messages, but active participants in the creation of meaning.

Adapted from Jenny Kitzinger (1997) 'Media influence', *Sociology Review*, Vol.6, No. 4.

(a) **Explain what is meant by a 'moral entrepreneur' (Item A).** (2 marks)

(b) **Give two examples of moral entrepreneurs.** (4 marks)

(c) **Suggest three ways in which advertisements may affect audiences.** (6 marks)

(d) **Identify and briefly explain two reasons why moral panics may occur.** (8 marks)

(e) **Examine the influence of practical issues and cultural influences on the selection and presentation of the news.** (20 marks)

(f) **With reference to the items and elsewhere, assess the view that 'audiences are passive recipients of predetermined messages'.** (20 marks)

Answer to question 4: grade-C candidate

(a) A moral entrepreneur is a businessman.

> 🖉 This is an incorrect response and does not score any marks.   **0/2 marks**

(b) Two examples are Richard Branson and Bill Gates.

> 🖉 Although in some capacity these men may have acted as moral entrepreneurs, it is not obvious that the candidate understands the term.   **0/4 marks**

(c) Ways that adverts may affect audiences are making them buy the products.

> 🖉 This is only one appropriate response to the question, which scores 2 marks.
>
>   **2/6 marks**

(d) Moral panics can occur for many different reasons. Here are two of them. Cohen researched mods and rockers in the 1960s and he found that there was a big panic over the way these groups behaved at the seaside. There were large mobs of mods and rockers chasing each other and causing damage. Because it was summertime there wasn't much news and so the story got printed and was exaggerated and caused people to have a moral panic.

> 🖉 The answer is not very well structured and the identifier is not made clear. However, we can take the summertime lack of news as an identifier, so the candidate scores 2 marks for this and 2 for the description.   **4/8 marks**

(e) The news is socially constructed by journalists and broadcasters. They have to gather all the news items together and sort through them to decide what is going to make up an edition of a newspaper or a television broadcast. This is not an easy process and they have a set of criteria to help them. Galtung and Ruge found these criteria when they researched newspapers. They called them news values.

> 🖉 This introduction demonstrates the socially constructed nature of news and introduces the concept of news values, but it is not yet directed to the essay question.

The question refers to practical issues and cultural influences, and news values relate to cultural influences. One of the news values is 'cultural relevance' which means how relevant the news item is to Britain. This is also called McLurg's Law. It means that if a disaster happens, like an air crash, and one Briton is on board, it will make the news, but if there are no Britons it might not make headline news. This was clear in the reporting of the Bali bombing. There were many British people involved and so it was a big news event. If there had only been Indonesians, it would not have run for such a long time. Another factor that helped to make it news was its negativity — it was about terrorism, which is very controversial at the moment. This aspect of news values is really ethnocentric. Other news values include reference to elite people and nations and personalisation. So if President

question

Bush is in the news, he stands for the American nation as well. Celebrities make the news, especially in the tabloid press where the news is usually about scandal and sensationalism.

> ✎ This paragraph focuses heavily on cultural influences at the expense of practical issues. It is often a good idea to use the actual terminology of the question as you answer it. This will keep your essay focused.

Practical issues are about things like space in the newspaper, the timing of an event and how much money is available for sending a news team abroad. Sometimes editors keep the headlines open if an event is about to occur like a royal birth. At other times they drop a headline story if something bigger happens.

> ✎ Again, it is evident that the candidate is most familiar with cultural influences, but there is at least reference to examples of practical issues.

There are different processes that are important as well. White argued that gatekeeping was important because editors were able to influence the selection of news with their own biases. Certain things are censored anyway by the Official Secrets Act, D notices and libel laws. Newspapers are afraid of being sued and are now more careful of what they print. Agenda-setting is also important as journalists and editors select items on the basis of the owner's politics. Most news takes a pro-management and pro-government line against the workers. This was the case with the miners' strike of 1984, as shown by the GMG. Marxists would say that the news was created in the interests of owners or of white middle-class men. We often get trivia as news to stop us seeing the real exploitation in society. But the pluralists would say that the news is produced in different ways to satisfy different audiences. News also comes from a wide range of sources, not just official ones, and therefore cannot be biased in a specific way.

> ✎ Although this paragraph is not particularly well structured, it deals with some relevant material.

It is difficult to say which of the two is more important. Practical issues are important for creating the news, but the content of the news is always related to agenda-setting, gatekeeping and news values and these all relate to cultural influences.

> ✎ This is a brief but evaluative conclusion that implicitly sees cultural influences as more relevant — a satisfactory ending to a sound essay. The candidate keeps to the question and a pleasing variety of knowledge and understanding is displayed.
>
> **14/20 marks**

(f) Item B says that some researchers have shown that audiences get 'pleasures' from the media and they can use the media and make their own interpretations from media texts. This is completely opposite to what the direct effects analysts say. They argue that audiences are injected with messages from the media and they behave according to the messages. For instance, the hypodermic needle approach sees the audience as completely passive and not able to control their behaviour. Some people argue that this is what happens when audiences watch advertisements, but buying products after watching adverts is not the same kind of behaviour as watching violent acts and becoming violent yourself.

🖉 The candidate makes use of Item B and clearly understands the direct effects model.

Instrumental Marxists also agree with this idea. They say that the proletariat are brainwashed by the media into believing that society is fair and good for them. All the ideas in the media simply benefit the bourgeoisie. Miliband said that the media were the new opium of the people, dulling their minds and stopping them understanding the true nature of their exploitation.

🖉 This paragraph develops the theoretical argument further and makes implicit use of the idea of predetermined messages.

Other researchers have shown that there are ways that audiences react to media texts, especially violent ones. The catharsis model says that if someone is angry or frustrated and then watches a television programme that reflects their situation, their own feelings disappear and they do not become aggressive. However, another effects model contradicts this and says that watching violence encourages our aggression. Some psychologists have shown that boys who watch a lot of violence become anti-social adults. The problem with this approach is that it ignores what happens to girls.

However, there are sociologists who completely reject the idea of the audience as passive recipients. Researchers like Buckingham and Morley argue that audiences are active and interpret the messages within media texts. Buckingham even says that children are active audiences of the media. So in answer to the question, recent media researchers reject the idea of passive audiences, but some theorists like the instrumentalist Marxists still argue that audiences are manipulated.

🖉 This is a sound answer that demonstrates a good grasp of direct effects models. The candidate has used AO2 skills effectively and has produced a balanced response.   **15/20 marks**

🖉 **Overall, the candidate would have done much better if questions (a) to (d) had been answered more carefully.**   **Overall: 35/60**

■ ■ ■

Answer to question 4: grade-A candidate

(a) A moral entrepreneur is someone like a church leader or a politician who wants to tell us what our moral position should be.

🖉 This is a good definition and gains full marks.   **2/2 marks**

(b) Mary Whitehouse, who started the National Viewers and Listeners Association to complain about sex and violence in the media, and the Archbishop of Canterbury.

✐ These examples demonstrate the candidate's correct understanding of the concept.

4/4 marks

(c) Three ways that advertisements may affect audiences are: by making them consume the products shown, by giving them more information, e.g. for insurance policies and pensions, and by helping them to choose between brands based on the different 'qualities' of the products shown.

✐ This is a sound response. The candidate has understood the question and given appropriate suggestions. **6/6 marks**

(d) One of the reasons for moral panics according to Goode and Ben Yehuda is the elite-engineered explanation. In this case elite groups use the event as a diversion away from 'real issues' that might be actual crises, as Hall et al. argued in *Policing the Crisis*.

The other explanation they give is the grassroots model. In this case it is the people on the street who start the panic, not politicians and the media. Parents may be concerned about their children finding syringes left in the neighbourhood and a panic over drug-taking in that area might start.

✐ This is a well-informed response, citing a key text (and in this way possibly gaining an advantage over students who are not familiar with it) that scores full marks for each model mentioned. It would also be appropriate to use the deviancy amplification model here. What other possibilities can you think of? **8/8 marks**

(e) The selection of the news is a subject that many sociologists disagree on. The ideas of what are 'practical issues' vary between each sociological perspective.

Pluralists would agree that the news tackles practical issues that concern the cultural influences on the population as a whole. They believe that the presentation of news reflects the interests of society in general and, as such, would cover a broad range from trivia and gossip to international stories. The selection is fair and just, and the media work in the interests of everyone.

✐ The candidate hasn't clearly discussed the meaning of practical issues. The question requires reference to time, space and funds.

However, Marxists would criticise this view as naive. They see the mass media as a manipulative device in the hands of those who own the processes of production. The content of the media is broadcast in their interests; the aim is not to rock the boat. The ideological messages of the media and, therefore, also of the news involve pacification of the working class and the importance of a false consciousness that doesn't challenge the status quo.

✐ This is a good theoretical paragraph that challenges the ideas of pluralists discussed earlier in the essay.

Regarding the preparation and selection of the news, Marxists would say there is more of a cultural influence upon this process, but that this cultural influence is negative and coercive as it is that of the dominant class. The journalists who work under the rule of the editor have their stories selected on the basis of the dominant ideology. Stories that show the dominant class or ruling government in a critical light are omitted, and this ability for setting the agenda keeps its audience in the dark about real political and social issues.

The candidate has a sound grasp of the instrumentalist Marxist position, even though the term is not used.

Some people believe that the media are supposed to be impartial, and news selection and presentation should reflect this impartiality, but who determines 'practical issues'? The Glasgow Media Group carried out several studies — *Bad News, More Bad News, Really Bad News* — which investigated the ways in which news was presented, with close attention to the handling of strikes by unionists. Its findings revealed a bias in favour of the managers and against the unionists. Often this was simply a matter of the language used to describe the 'negotiations': the unionists 'demanded' and 'insisted' whereas the managers 'pleaded'. There was also a preoccupation with the amount of money that the strike was costing the firm and so all of this helped to show the workers in a negative light. The Glasgow Media Group showed that the cultural influences of the dominant class strongly and deliberately affect news selection and presentation.

This is a well-focused paragraph giving sociological evidence for cultural factors in the argument.

The notion of hegemony is a strong one with regard to the selection and presentation of news. The average journalist is a white, middle-class male and while journalists may try to retain impartiality, it is inevitable that some of their dominant ideology should pervade the news. The news selected is likely to concern the middle class, have a racist slant and even be opposed to the working class, but this is not necessarily, as the Marxists would suggest, a consciously manipulative reproduction of dominant ideology. The hegemonic theorists press the notion that this is a subconscious result.

Again, the candidate makes good use of theory and links it to substantive evidence.

Marxist theorists would agree that stories about the royal family are deliberately included by the media as an ideological means of getting the working class to accept the hierarchy and even to respect it. In addition, by running stories or news bulletins on the royals, the dominant class avoids more serious political issues. This is the idea of bread and circuses that the Frankfurt School of Marxists follow.

There is pleasing evidence here that the candidate appreciates the importance of cultural factors such as the newsworthiness of the royal family.

The three main perspectives on the media put different emphases on the notion of 'practical issues' and 'cultural theory'. The pluralist perspective would argue that the practical issues are probably more dominant in the selection of news, but it is the cultural influence of value consensus that deems these issues practical. The hegemonic theorists argue that 'seemingly' practical issues are culturally influenced in a subconscious manner by the journalists themselves.

> ✑ Few candidates would be able to produce an essay this long within the time constraints. Although the candidate has covered a wide range of issues, the answer has not really addressed the issue of practical factors — in fact, the candidate may have misread the question as 'impartial' factors. However, the sophistication in presenting the evidence for cultural factors is extremely pleasing and mature and would score highly. **17/20 marks**

(f) The idea that the audience is passive comes from the instrumentalist Marxists who say that we are all taken in by the messages of the media that are simply put there by the ruling class to keep us in a state of false consciousness so that we do not have a revolution. Miliband said that television was the new opium of the masses.

> ✑ This is a sound introduction and unusually takes a theoretical stance from the outset.

Item B refers to the work of the Centre for Contemporary Cultural Studies and its argument is that audience members are the opposite of passive — they are 'active participants in the creation of meaning'. What this means is that the audience does not act like a cultural dope as the direct effects researchers used to argue, but rather that the audience interprets media messages all the time.

> ✑ Reference is made to the item and a good interpretation is offered. The candidate gains marks for AO2 skills by analysing, interpreting and identifying the extract.

Stuart Hall referred to audiences making different readings of texts. He said that there were three ways that we can read media messages: dominant, which is the way producers want us to read it; negotiated, where we make sense of it for ourselves; and oppositional, where we reject the messages. Morley found this with the black students watching *Nationwide*, who said that the programme was not about them and so they did not want to watch it.

In *Seeing is Believing* the GMG found that not everyone accepted the definitions of the miners' strike that were given by the media and the politicians. Those who had experienced the strike or who knew people involved were more 'realistic' in the way they described the events. This is the difference between mediated and situational reality. People who have no experience of an event or place etc. will accept the media's view. This is called mediated reality. However, if you have experienced something for yourself then that is situational reality. This was shown in Gerbner's work on cultivation analysis. Those who were heavy viewers accepted the mediated reality and saw a mean world, whereas those who were light viewers had a situational reality position and were not as negative as the others.

🖉 There is some good analysis of supporting evidence here. Evaluation is also woven into the response.

Although this research is quite dated, it has influenced the more recent work of the reception analysts. Buckingham and others say that the audience is active and even children are media literate.

🖉 The essay lacks a conclusion and comes to rather an abrupt end. Although the candidate has a sound grasp of the area, a conclusion is needed to gain a really high mark.   **15/20 marks**

🖉 **In all of these answers the candidate has demonstrated a sophisticated knowledge and understanding as well as a range of AO2 skills.**

Overall: 52/60

News, representation and audiences

Item A

Globalisation is the process whereby large corporations operate on an increasingly worldwide scale. Today many media industries operate as transnational corporations. Some corporations developed internationally quite early on whereas others have become involved more recently. Some of the news agencies, such as Reuters, have global connections. News International operates globally and Murdoch has many diverse media interests, some of which he has to protect against the interests of others that he owns. For instance, he managed to stop the publication of a book by a former British governor of Hong Kong that was possibly critical of China. This was seen as an attempt to protect his negotiations with China for entry into the Chinese media market.

Item B

Reception analysis is one of the more recent ways in which media researchers view the relationship between audiences and the media. However, it is not completely new. It emerges from earlier approaches such as uses and gratifications and reinforcement theory, both of which viewed audiences as active agents. Reception analysis takes this argument a step further by maintaining that children are also active viewers who are, from an early age, media literate. Researchers who adopt this approach look at the interpretations viewers make of television programmes, showing that different people in the audience will read the same media text in very different ways depending on their personal subjectivities.

(a) **Explain what is meant by the term 'transnational corporation' (Item A).** (2 marks)

(b) **Identify two ways in which the media might promote the interests of global capitalism.** (4 marks)

(c) **Suggest three sources apart from news agencies from which newspapers get their information.** (6 marks)

(d) **Identify and briefly explain two features of the postmodernist approach to understanding the mass media.** (8 marks)

(e) **Examine the contribution of sociologists to understanding the ways in which the media portray disability and age.** (20 marks)

(f) **Using material from Item B and elsewhere, assess the view that audiences are powerful and media-literate.** (20 marks)

■ ■ ■

Answer to question 5: grade-C candidate

(a) A company like News International.

   🖉 This response contains only an example rather than a definition and therefore scores no marks.   **0/2 marks**

(b) One way is through advertising. Companies like Gap advertise across the world.

   🖉 The candidate only mentions one way, but it is correct.   **2/4 marks**

(c) Newspapers get their news from the general public and from official sources like the police and politicians.

   🖉 This gains 2 marks for general public and 2 for official sources. It does not, however, score any further marks as police and politicians are examples of official sources.   **4/6 marks**

(d) Marxists criticise the postmodernists for arguing that the traditional theories don't work any more, but Marxists say that you can't forget the power that the ruling class still has. Feminists say this is the same with the lack of importance the postmodernists place on gender inequalities, which they say still exist.

   🖉 This is a rather convoluted way of responding to the question. The candidate has given two criticisms, not features, of the approach. However, through these criticisms two features are actually outlined: traditional theories don't work any more and a lack of importance is given to gender. The candidate gains half marks for identifiers, but none for explanation.   **4/8 marks**

(e) Sociologists argue that the media portray both the disabled and old people in a negative way. Old people tend to be stereotyped as feeble and weak. Many sociologists say that we live in an ageist society and it is not valued to be old. On television old people are often seen as moaning and out of touch with the modern world, like Victor Meldrew in *One Foot in the Grave*. They are often seen as the victims of crime, and newspapers have presented the elderly as victims of 'granny bashing' and at risk of crime from young muggers.

   🖉 It appears that this candidate has taken age to mean old age — unless other groups are going to be mentioned later in the essay. However, some relevant evidence is produced here.

Tuchman said that old people are 'symbolically annihilated' by the media because they do not appear very often on television and when they do it isn't in a positive way. Harry Enfield's show had the 'old gits' and they were shown as very negative characters. However, you could criticise this idea because old women tend to be very powerful in soap operas. For Meehan they are portrayed as matriarchs and have a lot of power over their families, like Peggy Mitchell in *EastEnders*.

   🖉 There is evidence here and some evaluation. It is good to see that gender has been introduced as it cross-cuts age as a category.

question

The media also treat the disabled unfairly. Tom Shakespeare argues that there are three main stereotypes of the disabled. They are the evil, the 'super cripp' (like Stephen Hawkins who is very disabled but super-bright) and the pitied.

Traditionally, in many comics and films the disabled character was always the evil one. In Bond movies his enemies are often physically disabled and comics are full of evil, scarred individuals. There has been some research into the disabled, as Cumberbatch and Negrine have shown. It is mainly categories of the disabled on television. However, there is less research in this area than for gender and ethnicity. This may be because sociologists themselves are not that interested, as gender and ethnicity are more interesting topics.

> As suspected, this candidate has discussed the representation of only one age group: the elderly. If you answer a question of this kind, remember to address other age groups too. The essay could have been improved by the introduction of some theory, such as hegemonic Marxism. The work on disability is supported by useful references and there is an attempt at evaluation at the end, but the essay is brief and lacks a proper conclusion. **12/20 marks**

(f) Item B refers to the uses and gratifications approach. This is where the audience uses the media to satisfy certain needs. It was an approach started in the 1960s by Blumler and McQuail who did a lot of research asking people what programmes they watched and what their reasons for watching were. They then produced clusters of variables and showed that there were four needs — diversion, personal relationships, identity and surveillance. If people wanted to find out what was happening in the world they might watch current affairs programmes or even nature programmes. If they were lonely they might watch soaps for company. So the researchers showed that audiences were active and powerful — they could make choices. This is like the pluralist viewpoint which said that audiences use selective exposure, selective perception and selective retention. This means that people watch what they want to, they interpret things in the way that makes sense to them and they remember some things more than others.

> The candidate makes reference to the item, but has only selected the uses and gratifications approach so far. A fair understanding of the method and of the pluralist approach to audiences is demonstrated.

This was different from the direct effects model that said that the media were like a hypodermic syringe injecting people with messages and making them become violent. Bandura did experiments with small children. He made them watch adults hitting a Bobo doll with a mallet and then he said that the children imitated the adults and became violent. Huesmann, an American psychologist, also believed this and he said that boys who watched a lot of television would grow up to be bad drivers, and probably drunk and aggressive to their families.

> This paragraph challenges the active audience approach and examines — in a rather simplistic way — the direct effects position.

There are problems with the direct effects models because they assume that people are passive and will do anything that they see on television. If that were the case there would have been many more young people killing their parents after seeing *Natural Born Killers* and it was only one boy called Nathan Martinez and he said his father beat him with his belt. Another problem with the direct effects is that they are done in laboratories and this can't be the same as watching television at home. It is completely different watching in a lab with strangers and an experimenter and probably the children were quite shy and thought that they had to hit the doll.

🖉 Some evaluation of the direct effects approach is offered here. The material on the film *Natural Born Killers* is useful, as is the criticism of the laboratory method. However, the candidate's style is unsophisticated.

Sociologists do not like to use the lab method because it has demand characteristics and is artificial, so we cannot use the Bobo doll experiments for anything other than children in a lab situation.

This shows that the uses and gratifications approach sees the audience as not passive but active. The audience is powerful because it can make choices and is not manipulated like the Marxists argue.

🖉 There is some evaluation here and a limited conclusion that introduces a brief reference to Marxists. The candidate has failed to address the reference to reception analysis in the item, perhaps because he or she read it too quickly and failed to take in the points that were made. It is essential in these essays that you read any item material very closely. It might be useful to underline or highlight certain points so that you refer to them later in your essay. On the whole, this candidate makes some valid points about the passive audience.   **12/20 marks**

🖉 **The candidate loses marks on the first four questions and the essays omit some important material. Try them yourself in order to improve on them.**
     Overall: 34/60

■ ■ ■

Answer to question 5: grade-A candidate

(a) A transnational corporation is a company that carries out its business on a global scale. An example of this would be McDonald's.

🖉 This is a competent response and gains full marks.   **2/2 marks**

(b) One way might be by negative reporting of anti-capitalist demonstrations. The news tends to portray groups who protest at the economic summits as crazy anarchists who just enjoy causing trouble and doesn't really explain why they are protesting in the first place. Another way that the media might promote global capitalism is through advertising capitalist enterprises. Companies like Pepsi and Coca-Cola spend billions of dollars every year on marketing their products across the world.

Two sound ways that the media promote global capitalism are given together with explanations. **4/4 marks**

(c) News sources can be politicians and spokespeople for the royals or they can be ordinary members of the public.

 Three separately identified sources earn all 6 marks. **6/6 marks**

(d) Postmodernists have a very different view of the world from the earlier theorists like Marxists. In terms of mass media they see us living in a media-saturated world. The traditional view of class giving us our identity has now given way to pick and mix identities from the media and from the products we buy. They also argue that there has been a mixing of elite and popular culture. Classical music is no longer just for the elites, but is used for advertisements and often introduces sporting championships. Pavarotti sold many records of 'Nessun Dorma', which was the theme music to football.

 This is a sound response. Both of the features are identified and explained. **8/8 marks**

(e) Much of the representation of age in the media is linked to the ideology of ageism. This means negative feelings against a person or group because of their age. It is mainly used against those who are over retirement age. Hegemonic Marxists would say that ageism helps us to deal with the elderly in a marginalised way, and not to take them very seriously.

 This is a good introduction. It immediately links the question to ideology and theory and shows that the candidate is aware of various age groups, not just the elderly.

The ideology of age rests on biological characteristics and it ignores age as being socially constructed. However, age is not just about the elderly. Age groups are often shown in stereotypical ways. For example, children are presented mainly as innocents, but they are also the focus of concern about pester-power, where they watch adverts and pester their parents to buy. The most negative view of children has been as murderers of other children like the killers of Jamie Bulger and Damilola Taylor. Adolescents are represented as trouble, especially if they are male and black, as in the 'mugging crisis', but also if they are white, as with lager louts on holiday in Greece.

 This develops the first paragraph and introduces age as a social construction. The evidence is wide-ranging and sound.

Content analysis studies have shown that elderly women are under-represented compared with men, and there is traditional sex-role stereotyping. Men were also more likely to be portrayed with desirable traits, such as being active and clever. However, women were more likely to be given negative traits. In our society we tend to see old age as something that should be avoided. Youth is desirable but old age is not. In general, unless they are members of the elite, elderly people are 'symbolically annihilated' by the media, and older women get the worst deal — portrayed as witches or nagging wives.

> ☑ The candidate has included research evidence comparing men and women, again demonstrating the importance of gender in relation to age.

Disabled people are also shown in marginalised ways. Longmore has given a set of categories of the disabled on television. They include the disabled as evil, as monsters, as dependent mad, as courageous and as having super achievement to compensate for their disability. In early American thrillers, many of the 'baddies' were seen as disabled in some way and they were shown as frightening. Even in the *Batman* films, the Joker has a deformed face. Cumberbatch and Negrine have shown that the disabled are objects of pity, often in charity appeals. Very rarely are people shown as disabled where their disability is not an important part of their character. However, there have been a few adverts showing disabled people positively.

> ☑ This is sound evidence and makes reference to appropriate research.

In conclusion, the representations of age and disability fit into the hegemonic approach of marginalisation. Pluralists might challenge this by saying that things are getting better, but the progress is very slow.

> ☑ This is an excellent essay. It demonstrates a wide range of evidence which is referenced to sociological research. It deals with both age and disability, and if there is an imbalance in the coverage this can be forgiven as it reflects an imbalance in the research evidence. **18/20 marks**

(f) The relationship between the media and the audience outlined in Item B is that the audience is powerful and that viewers may interpret textual meanings differently from the ways that those meanings are encoded. However, other researchers have for a long time maintained that this is not the case and that the media can influence audiences and even have direct effects on them.

> ☑ The essay opens with a sound introductory paragraph that both addresses the item and interprets it.

Bandura and his researchers in the series of Bobo doll experiments wanted to find out if children were influenced by watching adults engaged in aggressive acts (in this case against a Bobo doll). The hypodermic syringe model was popular from the beginning of the twentieth century and Bandura's work is in this tradition. But the studies have been criticised as some children may not have taken them seriously and one child was overheard saying, 'Look Mummy, that's the doll we have to hit', showing that some children thought they were expected to imitate what they had seen.

> ☑ This paragraph takes on the argument from the direct effects approach and produces evidence of research studies from this perspective.

However, Katz and Lazarsfeld moved away from the media-centric approach in their research on the two-step flow hypothesis — the idea that an opinion leader in a social group, someone like a charismatic leader or an influential friend, would be more media active and pass on media messages to others. There is no reason why it should simply be only two steps, but the main criticism is that there is no method for discovering an opinion leader in the first place.

🖉 This paragraph demonstrates sound knowledge and understanding and it appears that the candidate is moving forward chronologically.

Closer to reception analysis was the uses and gratifications approach, which demonstrated that audiences had basic needs that were satisfied by the media. These were diversion and escapism, personal relationships, personal identity and surveillance. How the audience members satisfied these needs was a matter of individual taste. McQuail, Blumler and Brown identified the use of soap operas for personal relationships and personal identity. However, most of the researchers asked people to identify their needs after the event, not before. It is also a difficult task to justify your own media use.

The pluralist position is associated with the approach in Item B, as pluralists see audience members engaged in selective exposure, selective perception and selective retention. This means that people put themselves in front of different media, interpret those media in different ways and remember different aspects of what they have seen, read or heard.

🖉 This is again focused on the item and develops the pluralist position correctly. It is often a good idea to locate the studies in a theoretical framework as far as possible. This tells the examiner that you are able to make the links between theory and empirical evidence.

Item B refers to the 'subjectivities' of audiences. Fiske and Hartley have used this concept in order to show how people's social characteristics and experiences affect their reading of texts. This approach emerged from the ideas of dominant, negotiated and oppositional reading introduced by Stuart Hall and used by Morley in *The Nationwide Audience*. Although it moved the debate on from the earlier media-centric approaches, it was not made clear why particular audience groups took these positions and whether they were fixed readings for all media.

🖉 This is a very good section and uses entirely appropriate references to Hall and Morley.

To return to the idea of powerful audiences, the debate continues. It is interesting to see that Greg Philo has criticised the reception analysts for not taking account of how influential the media can be. They do not look at who makes programmes or who owns the press but concentrate only on meanings and interpretations of audiences without asking how the audience has access to these meanings in the first place. Children may be media literate, but that does not prevent them from being influenced, as 'pester power' shows us.

e This is an excellent closing paragraph. It is evaluative and also brings in a new viewpoint from Philo's work. Though long, the essay is well focused and the candidate has demonstrated very pleasing skills in all the assessed areas.

20/20 marks

e **The candidate demonstrates sound sociological understanding in these responses. The essays are coherent, evaluative and well developed.**

Overall: 58/60

Representation, deviancy amplification and news

Item A

The analysis of all television images involves the audience in a subjective, sense-making process. To understand the representations, we have to make sense of the codes and conventions of other cultural forms in which they are located. How we interpret the images depends on our own cultural background and experience; nevertheless, the viewing and reading codes available to us at any given time restrict us all. We are, therefore, helped to make sense of representations by reference to other similar images with which we are familiar. Representation of particular groups in the media is always limited by power relationships and ideology. If the majority of female, working-class and ethnic minority images have historically been stereotyped and marginalised it is because the media are dominated by a hegemonic culture that is white, male and middle class.

Adapted from: Marsha Jones and Matthew Jones (1996) 'Technoprimitives', *Sociology Review*, Vol. 5, No. 3.

Item B

The news is never impartial, objective truth, but media professionals — journalists and broadcasters — construct it according to a series of long-standing practices that they have learned. In a real sense the news could not exist without the mass media because events are filtered, selected, ordered and produced as a package of 'news'. Sociologists have observed the production of this process in television newsrooms and at newspaper offices. They have shown that what is produced as news is the result of negotiations between official sources, like governments, various pressure groups and sometimes the general public.

(a) Explain what is meant by the term 'marginalised' (Item A). (2 marks)

(b) Apart from those listed in Item A, identify two groups that have been marginalised by the media. (4 marks)

(c) Suggest three examples of news values. (6 marks)

(d) Identify and briefly explain two criticisms of the laboratory method to measure media effects. (8 marks)

(e) Examine the ways in which the mass media might cause the amplification of deviance. (20 marks)

(f) With reference to Item B and elsewhere, assess the view that the news is biased towards the interests of dominant groups. (20 marks)

■ ■ ■

Task This is a question for you to work through yourself. You should spend time looking through your notes and the relevant sections in this book. Try to time yourself: the examination lasts for 1 hour 15 minutes. Listed below are some guideline hints to help you.

(a) Try to produce a clear definition. You need to be familiar with hegemonic theory for this answer.

(b) As long as you have revised all the key concepts relating to the media, including marginalisation, you will be able to identify relevant groups.

(c) Here you simply need to provide three examples. Check the work of Galtung and Ruge for these.

(d) In your answers to questions like this, always identify *and* explain clearly so that you gain 2 + 2 marks for each criticism. You could think about artificiality, ethics, long-term and short-term effects, demand characteristics etc.

(e) In order to produce a good response to this question, you need to examine the relationship of the media as well as other agencies to the process of deviancy amplification. You might also introduce the debate about the effects of screen violence. You might challenge the idea that deviancy amplification actually exists outside the sociological literature. It was apparent that during and after the 'dangerous dogs' moral panic, many people came to view dogs such as pit bull terriers, Rottweilers and Alsatians as potentially harmful. It is important to consider whether the role of the media in amplifying deviance is exaggerated or not. Other agencies are also responsible, such as the police, courts and prisons. Examine their roles alongside that of the media.

(f) This is an opportunity to demonstrate your understanding of the news-making process: the role of official sources, the selection and filtering process associated with news values, and the agenda-setting and gatekeeping aspects of news-making. At a theoretical level you could compare the approaches of instrumentalists, hegemonic theorists and pluralists. Illustrate your arguments by looking at the way in which some social groups such as women, ethnic minorities and the disabled are stereotyped and marginalised by the media. You might also refer to the debate over press intrusion and the consequent changes in privacy legislation. Don't forget that this essay is weighted towards AO2 skills. You must demonstrate your skills of identification, interpretation and, especially, analysis and evaluation.